Sensibility

Sensibility
An introduction

Janet Todd

Methuen · London & New York

For George and Elizabeth Dakin
and in memory of Edna V. Jones

First published in 1986 by
Methuen & Co. Ltd
11 New Fetter Lane,
London EC4P 4EE

Published in the USA by
Methuen & Co.
in association with Methuen, Inc.
29 West 35th Street,
New York NY 10001

© 1986 Janet Todd

Set by Hope Services, Abingdon
Printed in Great Britain by
Richard Clay (The Chaucer Press) Ltd,
Bungay, Suffolk

*British Library Cataloguing in
Publication Data*
Todd, Janet
Sensibility: an introduction.
1. English literature – 18th century –
History and criticism   2. English
literature – 19th century – History
and criticism
3. Sentimentalism in literature
I. Title
820.9   PR449.S4
ISBN 0 416 37710 6
      0 416 37720 3 Pbk

*Library of Congress Cataloging-in-
Publication Data*
Todd, Janet M. 1942–
Sensibility: an introduction.
Bibliography: p.
Includes index.
1. English literature – 18th century –
History and criticism.
2. Sentimentalism in literature.
I. Title.
PR449.S4T63   1986   820′.9′353
86–5314
ISBN 0 416 37710 6
      0 416 37720 3 (pbk.)

Contents

Acknowledgements

I should like to thank Barry Nisbet, Paul Russell, Marilyn Butler, William St Clair, James Lynn and John Mullan for helpful conversations and criticism. I am also grateful to Sidney Sussex College for its support of my work.

I *Introduction*

'Oh! my children, my children,' he cried, 'have I found you thus? My poor Jack, art thou gone? I thought thou shouldst have carried thy father's grey hairs to the grave! and these little ones' – his tears choked his utterance, and he fell again on the necks of the children.

'My dear old man,' said Harley, 'Providence has sent you to relieve them; it will bless me if I can be the means of assisting you.'

'Yes, indeed, sir,' answered the boy; 'father, when he was a-dying bade God bless us, and prayed that if grandfather lived he might send him to support us.'

'Where did they lay my boy?' said Edwards.

'In the Old Churchyard,' replied the woman, 'hard by his mother.'

'I will show it you,' answered the boy, 'for I have wept over it many a time when first I came among strange folks.'

He took the old man's hand, Harley laid hold of his sister's, and they walked in silence to the churchyard.

There was an old stone, with the corner broken off, and some letters, half-covered with moss, to denote the names of the dead:

there was a cyphered R. E. plainer than the rest; it was the tomb they sought.

'Here it is, grandfather,' said the boy.

Edwards gazed upon it without uttering a word: the girl, who had only sighed before, now wept outright; her brother sobbed, but he stifled his sobbing.

'I have told sister,' said he, 'that she should not take it so to heart; she can knit already, and I shall soon be able to dig, we shall not starve, sister, indeed we shall not, nor shall grandfather neither.'

The girl cried afresh; Harley kissed off her tears as they flowed, and wept between every kiss.[1]

The sacred names of friend, father, lover, husband, son, mother, of mankind in general, these are far more pathetic than aught else and retain their claims for ever. What matters the rank, the surname, the genealogy of the unfortunate man whose easy good nature towards unworthy friends has involved him in gambling and who loses over this his wealth and honour and now sighs in prison distracted by shame and remorse? If asked, who is he? I reply: He was an honest man and, to add to his grief, he is a husband and a father; his wife, whom he loves and who loves him, is suffering extreme need and can only give tears to the children who clamour for bread. Show me in the history of heroes a more touching, a more moral, indeed a more tragic situation! And when at last this miserable man takes poison and then learns that Heaven had willed his release, what is absent, in this painful, terrible moment, when to the horrors of death are added the tortures of imagination, telling him how happily he could have lived – what, I say, is absent to render the situation worthy of a tragedy? The wonderful, will be replied. What! Is there not matter wonderful enough in this sudden change from honour to shame, from innocence to guilt, from sweet peace to despair; in brief, in the extreme misfortune into which mere weakness has plunged him![2]

The arousal of pathos through conventional situations, stock familial characters and rhetorical devices is the mark of sentimental literature. Such literature buttonholes the reader and demands an emotional, even physical response.

The sentimental work reveals a belief in the appealing and

aesthetic quality of virtue, displayed in a naughty world through a vague and potent distress. This distress is rarely deserved and is somehow in the nature of things; in later sentimental works it even overshadows virtue, which may in fact be more manifest in the sympathy of the observer than in the sufferer. The distressed are natural victims, whose misery is demanded by their predicament as defenceless women, aged men, helpless infants or melancholic youths.

The works inhabited by these unfortunates require no decon-structing – although they may affectionately mock aspects of themselves – and they discourage multiple readings. They provoke tears in a way no other literature does. The tears that may be shed at high or heroic tragedy form part of a complex intellectual and emotional response, but, when sentimental works are accepted and in fashion, they primarily make the reader or watcher cry. If they become outmoded, such works seem ridiculous: the first excerpt above is from *The Man of Feeling*, published in 1771 in the middle of the high period of sensibility, when it met a public hungry for sentimental scenes and emotionally prepared to receive them; a few decades later, it was ignored or greeted with embarrassed laughter.

The sentimental impulse is recurrent in literature. Pathetic and sensationally moving elements involving domestic relationships and distressed virtue exist in the Greek drama of Euripides for example, in medieval morality plays and, most obviously, in the Elizabethan and Jacobean drama of Fletcher, Heywood and Shirley. Pathos resulting from the sudden intrusion of the child-and-parent tie is aroused in Shakespeare's *Antony and Cleopatra* when the asp becomes a baby at the breast and 'sucks the nurse asleep', and in *King Lear* when Lear imagines retreat into a blissful domestic prison with Cordelia. But these pathetic elements remain subordinate to other concerns of plot and character. What is new in the eighteenth century is the centrality of sentiment and pathos.

A further difference from the works of earlier periods derives from the alliance in interests of eighteenth-century literature and moral philosophy. In the early years, philosophy both responded to and created a popular demand for a new set of ideas with which to account for human nature and order society, beyond the expla-nations given by Christian dogma. Through literature and the popularizations of moral philosophy, sentimental theory and art became extremely widespread in England, touching the perceptions of most literate and semi-literate people.

Sentimentalism entered all literary genres – the novel, essay, poetry and drama. But the cult of sensibility was largely defined by fiction from the 1740s to the 1770s. This fiction initially showed people how to behave, how to express themselves in friendship and how to respond decently to life's experiences. Later, it prided itself more on making its readers weep and in teaching them when and how much to weep. In addition, it delivered the great archetypal victims: the chaste suffering woman, happily rewarded in marriage or elevated into redemptive death, and the sensitive, benevolent man whose feelings are too exquisite for the acquisitiveness, vulgarity and selfishness of his world.

In all forms of sentimental literature, there is an assumption that life and literature are directly linked, not through any notion of a mimetic depiction of reality but through the belief that the literary experience can intimately affect the living one. So literary conventions become a way of life. At the same time literary emotions herald active ones; a theatrical or fictional feeling creates greater virtue in the audience or reader, and a contrived tear foreshadows the spontaneous one of human sympathy. Sentimental literature is exemplary of emotion, teaching its consumers to produce a response equivalent to the one presented in its episodes. It is a kind of pedagogy of seeing and of the physical reaction that this seeing should produce, clarifying when uncontrolled sobs or a single tear should be the rule, or when the inexpressible nature of the feeling should be stressed.

A sentimental work moralizes more than it analyses and emphasis is not on the subtleties of a particular emotional state but on the communication of common feeling from sufferer or watcher to reader or audience. The work may include a constructed sentimental author, but it rarely points back to a particular individual artist whose artistry constitutes his greatness.

The techniques of sentimentalism vary according to genre and time, but most works function through a plot of sudden reversal – the second passage above, by Marmontel on Edward Moore's *The Gamester*, will illustrate – whether these are large narrative events like the sudden loss of a newly rediscovered child or the psychological changes when a contrasting mood or thought interrupts a burgeoning emotion. All present these contrasts and the exemplary emotion in tableaux, usually drawing on the notion of the family unit or the reclusive individual; when they occur, the story or argument is arrested so that the author can conventionally intensify the emotion and the reader or spectator may have time physically to respond.

The words in which emotion is described and prescribed are themselves prescribed. Terms such as 'benevolence', 'virtue', 'esteem', 'delicacy', and 'transport' indicate sentimental doctrine and expect a sentimental understanding. The word 'weakness', for example, moves from Johnson's dictionary definition of 'want of judgment . . . foolishness of mind' to suggest a pardonable excess of some quality in which a sentimentalist might have pride, like tenderness or pity. In general, vocabulary in a sentimental work is conventional, repetitive, mannered and overcharged. It is also hyperbolic; a few adjectives such as the eulogistic 'sweet', 'grateful' and 'delicate', and constructions such as 'the best of mothers' do much service, as do the pejoratives, 'cruel' and 'base', and the negatives 'unkind', 'ungenerous' and 'unfeeling', which, as Erik Erämetsä observes in his study of sentimental vocabulary, emphasize the goodness they negate.[3]

The association of nouns and adjectives is predictable – the heart is 'kind', 'honest', 'tender' and 'fond'; feeling is 'melting', 'swelling' or 'overflowing', and sighs and tears are 'pitying' and 'sympathetic'. Adjectives gain intensity through the prefixes 'over', 'ever' and 'all', as in 'all-conquering', and through the adverbs 'vastly' and 'exceedingly', much mocked by Jane Austen's Henry Tilney in *Northanger Abbey*. Terms and structures are repeated to heighten intensity – 'cruel, thrice cruel' – and words come in pairs or triplets, underlining the point and preventing much attention to any individual term: 'griefs and suffering' or 'sincere, honest and open'.

In the sentimental work words are not left to carry a message alone, but are augmented by other heightening devices. Exclamation marks, brackets, italics and capitals pepper and disturb the flow of sentences. At the same time they are shunted into declaring their inadequacy and their subordination to gesture. A physical reaction may, for example, be conveyed through a description which is made deficient or foolish because of the sheer number of words needed to contain what was instantaneous. Or it may be given through typographical devices stressing the absence of words and so the presence of other methods of communication. A work such as Richardson's *Clarissa* is full of lacunae, asterisks, dashes and disturbed or aberrant typography, indicating emotion beyond words, presumably in imitation of the communication of penmanship which the printed novel cannot deliver. In the extreme case of *Tristram Shandy*, black and marbled pages are substituted for verbal descriptions.

Because sensibility is reactive and unstable, the sentimental work of prose or poetry meanders rather than moves logically to its destination. Or it may have no destination at all and pretend to be, or actually be, unfinished. Again this is taken to an extreme in Sterne: in *Tristram Shandy* characters and fictive narrator ride the hobby-horses of their ideas so hard that the book can never overtake the passing moment; *A Sentimental Journey Through France and Italy by Mr Yorick* breaks off with the clutching hand of the narrator who never sets foot in Italy.

The novels of Richardson, Mackenzie, Sterne and a host of women writers of the late eighteenth century declare themselves fragmented. Gaps are written into the works through the pretence of missing chapters, torn sentences or mutilated letters. The poetry of Gray and Thomson is similarly broken by hiatuses, seeming closures and juxtapositions of conflicting points of view and contrary moods.

The result of these various devices – asterisks, dashes, meandering narrative and fragmentation – is that readers are to some extent prevented from indulging in an identifying fantasy with a character or an author and are forced to respond to the emotion conveyed. At the same time these devices force the literary nature of the work on to the reader by indicating the inadequacy of the medium – language – in which, despite their intrusive presence, most of the business of the work is still transacted.

Terms

The terms 'sentiment', 'sensibility', 'sentimentality', and 'sentimentalism' are counters in eighteenth-century literature and philosophy, sometimes representing precise formulations and sometimes vaguely suggesting emotional qualities. They were at home in the scientific or epistemological treatise and in the familiar letter. Often such terms were used interchangeably. It is possible, however, to extricate 'sentimentalism'. Once employed only pejoratively to suggest affectation and excessive emotional display, it was used by Sir Leslie Stephen in *English Thought in the Eighteenth Century* as 'the name of the mood in which we make a luxury of grief'.[4] More recently the word has come to denote the movement discerned in philosophy, politics and art, based on the belief in or hope of the natural goodness of humanity and manifested in a humanitarian concern for the unfortunate and helpless.

Often in literary criticism 'sentiment' and 'sensibility' are felt to be synonymous, a novel of sentiment differing in no way from a novel of sensibility. But there is, none the less, a useful distinction to be made in historical usage and reference. A 'sentiment' is a moral reflection, a rational opinion usually about the rights and wrongs of human conduct; the early eighteenth-century novel of sentiment is characterized by such generalized reflections. But a 'sentiment' is also a thought, often an elevated one, influenced by emotion, a combining of heart with head or an emotional impulse leading to an opinion or a principle. James Thomson's 'melting sentiments of kindly care', for example, are clearly expressions of a feeling heart as well as a reflecting mind. In this case 'sentiment' comes close to 'sensibility', which also presupposes an emotional susceptibility. After Sterne's novels, it frequently takes the meaning of refined and tender emotion, although the denotation of moral reflection also continues.

'Sensibility' is perhaps the key term of the period. Little used before the mid-eighteenth century, although Addison among others had employed it to suggest delicate emotional and physical susceptibility, it came to denote the faculty of feeling, the capacity for extremely refined emotion and a quickness to display compassion for suffering. Its adjectives tell the tale of its rise and fall. It is 'exquisite' in Addison, 'delicate' in Hume, 'sweet' in Cowper, and 'dear' in Sterne. But as it declines from fashion, it becomes 'acute' in Austen, 'trembling'. in Hazlitt, 'mawkish' in Coleridge, and 'sickly' in Byron. In the 1760s and 1770s many poems extol sensibility, while in the 1780s and 1790s book titles such as *Excessive Sensibility* become common.

'Sensibility', an innate sensitiveness or susceptibility revealing itself in a variety of spontaneous activities such as crying, swooning and kneeling, is defined in 1797 by the *Encyclopaedia Britannica* (3rd edn) as 'a nice and delicate perception of pleasure or pain, beauty or deformity', which, as far as it is natural, 'seems to depend upon the organization of the nervous system'. Here it appears physically based, a quality of nerves turning easily to illness and described in contemporary medical treatises in terms of movements within the body.

The cult of sensibility that jangled the nerves of Europe in the mid-eighteenth century is the cultural movement devoted to tear-demanding exhibitions of pathos and unqualified virtue. In literature it was notably expressed in the novels of Sterne, Mackenzie, Rousseau and Goethe, in the melancholic poetry of Young and Gray, in English drama from Steele and Cibber to Cumberland and Kelly, and in French *comédie larmoyante* of Nivelle de la Chaussée. It was also manifested in the religious dread of James Hervey among the 'thickening Shades' of the graveyard, where tender innocence cannot be stained by the world.[5]

In his *L'Homme machine* (1747) La Mettrie associated sexuality and sensibility, seeing the mind and body as different forms of the same substance, and many less systematic thinkers, considering sensibility as moral and physical susceptibility, inevitably found sexuality a component: Tom Jones's robust and Yorick's whimsical sexuality feed into and derive from their sensibility. This was not, however, openly felt to be the case with women, in whom sensibility, when admired, was assumed to imply chastity, and only if denigrated was feared to denote sexuality. As sensibility became more firmly connected with women in the later eighteenth century, it tended to lose the association with sexuality even for men, and the sensibility of the Man of Feeling is physically a matter of tears and gestures, precluding lustiness.

The novel of sentiment of the 1740s and 1750s praises a generous heart and often delays the narrative to philosophize about bene-volence; the novel of sensibility, increasingly written from the 1760s onwards, differs slightly in emphasis since it honours above all the capacity for refined feeling. It stops the story to display this feeling in the characters and elicit it in the reader in its physical manifestations of tears and trembling. Such display is justified by the belief that a heightened sense of one's virtue through pity for another is morally improving.

'Sentimentality' came in as a pejorative term in the 1770s when the idea of sensibility was losing ground. It suggested and still suggests debased and affected feeling, an indulgence in and display of emotion for its own sake beyond the stimulus and beyond propriety. In France where 'sensibilité' translated the English sensibility, a new term 'sensiblerie' developed to distinguish sensibility from the debased and self-indulgent quality.

The adjective 'sentimental' is the cause of much of the confusion of terms. It does duty for all the nouns so far mentioned – 'sentiment', 'sentimentalism', 'sensibility', and 'sentimentality' – and cannot discriminate amongst them. Its vagueness was there at its inception, for in 1749 Lady Bradshaigh wrote to Samuel Richardson: 'Pray, Sir, give me leave to ask you (I forgot it before) what, in your opinion, is the meaning of the word *sentimental*.' She notes that it seems used for 'everything clever and agreeable'.[6] After the publication of *A Sentimental Journey* in 1768, she would probably have been given a response very different from her assumption in the 1740s, but perhaps it would have been as imprecise, since the term appeared to imply all that was elevated and aesthetically pleasing in feeling, all that appealed to and expressed the finer emotions, and all that was morally refined. Before Sterne used it in his title, the noun of 'sentimental' was commonly 'sentiment' and it suggested richness in moral reflection; after his use, it tended more often to apply to sensibility and its emotional and physical manifestations, and to indicate the heart rather than the head.

In 1775 the playwright George Colman the Elder lamented that 'sentimental' had come to suggest dull moralities, while by 1800 its use was commonly pejorative; it was tied both to despised sentimentality and to discredited sensibility. In present usage, except when employed critically to denote a historical genre such as 'sentimental comedy', a usage dating from the 1750s, it has welded itself firmly to sentimentality.

Although it had its heyday from the 1740s to the late 1770s, the literature of sensibility is not discrete. Sentimental elements increase in importance through Restoration tragedy and early eighteenth-century comedy, and after the 1770s they also inhabit Gothic fiction and Romantic poetry. And yet sentimental literature is distinct from primarily Romantic or Gothic works. If, as Schlegel argues in an early definition, Romanticism includes a depiction of 'emotional matter in an imaginative form', the emphasis on 'imaginative' makes a discrimination, for such individual expression is far from the deliberate clichés of sentimental writing and its common social concern.[7] Gothic fiction, emerging in the 1760s but growing fashionable only in the 1790s, uses sentimental contrasts of virtue and vice or malignancy and distressed worth, but goes far towards sensationalizing and often sexualizing these elements, while it retreats from the didactic aim of sentimental literature.

II *Historical Background*

Sentimentalism is associated with a variety of social and cultural phenomena: the shifting importance of various classes, the growth of London, the increase in publishing and literary activity in the provincial towns, the changing perception of the family and its importance within society, the economic and cultural situation of women, and the interrelated developments in religion, philosophy and science. There is no hard association or simple cause and effect among these elements: for instance sentimentalism is frequently connected with the middle or trading classes and with Dissent and reform, yet it seems as clearly fascinated with aristocracy's effortless privilege and contempt for trade; sentimental techniques and their appreciation can be discerned in Anglican, Independent, conservative and radical alike. It is, then, a matter of emphasis and number, not of complete identification and opposition.

Class

The Glorious Revolution of 1688 established William of Orange on the throne of England in place of the mystic Stuart kings. His arrival largely deprived kingship and aristocratic hierarchy of their divinity; a basic equality was, from that time onwards, felt ideally to obtain in the state, even if politically it was little in evidence.

One group that benefited by this establishment was the Dissenters, whose partial liberty it guaranteed but whose yearning for complete civil rights it failed to meet. Throughout the eighteenth century the Dissenters were a force for political reform and, while the development of their religious beliefs was in the main away from sentimental and towards rational faith, their libertarian concerns were reinforced by the sentimental interest in the deprived. The most famous Dissenting divines rarely wrote sentimental literature, but they were certainly its consumers, and they encouraged many to produce it.

The change indicated by the Glorious Revolution was further developed by the Hanoverian succession of 1714 when the last of the reigning Stuarts died. Other Stuarts threatened the state in 1715 and 1745, but the threat was speedily contained and the rebels were soon sentimentalized into literary folk heroes, suitable subjects for melancholy ballads and tales.

The coming of the Hanoverians provided political stability and appeared to denote a shift in class power. Although England was, beyond any consideration of Whig or Tory, ruled by an aristocratic élite, the power of the middle and trading classes was felt to be increasing. Money was a factor of considerable importance in politics and society, and, although a rise in the world was still ratified by land ownership, the rise itself often resulted from trade. The thrusting merchant with the Dissenting values of individualism, personal effort and domestic piety, holding a mercantile philosophy of competition and probity, was a frequent character in early literature containing sentimental elements; in 1722 Mr Sealand in Steele's *The Conscious Lovers* (1722) could boast, 'we Merchants are a species of Gentry, that have grown into the World this last Century, and are as honourable, and almost as useful, as you landed Folks, that have always thought yourselves so much above us'.

In life, however, the classes were not so clearly distinct. The aristocratic oligarchy was reinforced by the bourgeoisie, and the alliance of city money and aristocratic property could produce the huge landscaped estates so much a feature of eighteenth-century England. The business class reared leisured children whose way of life aped the image of the aristocrat. Later sentimental literature spoke to this leisure and often presented the commercial classes less with images of mercantile probity and benevolence than with an ideal of rural escape and unproductive bliss.

The greater importance of the middle class in literary consumption suggested a relationship of author and reader different from the patronage by aristocrat of artist. With Charles II had come a noble court, frivolous from exile and exaggeratedly urbane and cynical beside the serious Puritans it ousted. The literature of this court was witty, topical and knowing, and it assumed classical learning and social knowledge in its readers. But, as the eighteenth century progressed, there grew a larger, less educated market not requiring the individual attention of an artist and so severing the personal tie of author and reader. Circulating libraries, beginning in the first quarter, increased substantially in the 1740s and continued to grow throughout the century. Books could therefore be cheaply procured and they became more clearly a consumer commodity. In the next century this state of affairs troubled the artist who felt alienated through ignorance of the reading public. In the eighteenth century, however, it provoked an excited self-consciousness, an effort by writers to construct readers for themselves and an awareness of writing as a theatrical performance in a darkened auditorium.

Judging from the publications of the late seventeenth and early eighteenth centuries, the growing classes wanted instruction as well as entertainment, but they wanted it along more obvious and practical lines than the earlier spiritual handbooks and doctrinal allegories had been delivering. To some extent they found this instruction in new periodicals like the *Tatler* and the *Spectator* and in manuals of social advice. The serious and practical temper of the times can be gauged from such productions and from the reforming societies that developed during these years – for promoting Christian knowledge, for improving morals and manners, and for purifying the stage.

The most public literary genre, drama, registers the desire for ethical instruction. In 1704 Colley Cibber wrote *The Careless Husband* which seemed to many a sermon with a plot. Its Prologue stated that his plays aimed 'with Breeding to refine the Age,/ To chasten Wit, and Moralize the Stage'. In 1740, even more categorically, Cibber declared himself an entirely moralizing dramatist in total opposition to 'a licentious Theatre'.

Writers in – as opposed to later scholars of – the eighteenth century had some difficulty relating class and sensibility. Sometimes they saw sensibility as equalizing since it occurred in all ranks; at other times they considered it a property more or less exclusively of the higher and more genteel orders. The former view insisted on a meritocracy of feeling not necessarily coinciding with the hierarchy of birth. An uneasiness at this is gently mocked by Thomas Monroe in *Olla Podrida* (15, 23 June 1787), when he claimed that 'no man should be permitted to moisten a white handkerchief at the *ohs* and *ahs* of a modern tragedy, unless he possessed an estate of seven hundred a year'. Bishop Hurd suggested that the capacity to react sentimentally was peculiar to people of birth and culture, while Hannah More's poem 'Sensibility' denied sentimental pensiveness to the vulgar. In *The First Floor* (1787), James Cobb presents sentiment as a gratification of the over-monied and leisured: 'What's become of the exquisite luxury of a feeling mind in relieving distress?' asks a young gentleman and is answered by the tradesman: 'It may do very well for people of fortune, but a tradesman should never indulge in luxury'; generosity is a 'losing trade . . . therefore it shan't be a part of *my* business'.

One area that suggests the complexity of the class alignment with sensibility is the attitude of the employing classes to servants. Employers in the eighteenth century were sure that they had a servant problem, and there is much perturbation about the insubordination and mercenariness of domestics. It seemed to many that the older quasi-feudal tie of master and man had been broken and that, as servants became more mobile and independent, they were forming a class of their own, no longer coinciding in interest with their masters. By mid-century there was much worldly acceptance that, as one writer expressed it, 'servants have very little attachment to those they serve . . . self is the sole motive'.[1]

But, to compensate for this fear of solidarity and awareness of conflicting interest, the employing classes seem to have indulged, through sentimental literature, in a fantasy of service as familial and feudal, a fantasy which they sometimes expected to find embodied in life. So, alongside the abuse of servants, a literature flourished which presented service as an ideal sentimental community and the servant ties as filial and parental. James Hanway's tract, *Virtue in Humble Life* (1774), was prefaced by a picture of Mary bathing Christ's feet; it included affecting pictures of servants willing to live and die for those they served. In the fiction of Sterne the tie of master and man overtops in sentimental display anything lovers can produce, as it does again in the Gothic novels of Ann Radcliffe:

> 'It is my master! It is my dear master!' cried Paolo, [the faithful servant of Vivaldi], and, fending off a nobleman with each elbow, as he made his way between them, he hugged Vivaldi in his arms, repeating, 'O, my master! My master!' till a passion of joy and affection overcame his voice, and he fell at his master's feet and wept.'[2]

Here sensibility is displayed in the lower orders, but only through their tie with the master in a fantastic aristocratic world.

Location

Throughout the eighteenth century, London dominated the literary scene. It was the locus of commerce and the court as well as of publishing and bookselling. In the years of peace and successful war, it grew large and prosperous, at least for the richer classes. Restoration comedy set itself firmly in London, and the idea of Hampshire chilled the soul of Harriet in *The Man of Mode* (1676).

The Augustans of the early decades felt themselves Londoners, as did the later circle of Johnson, Reynolds, Goldsmith and Burke, although none of these men was born there; associated with the ruling establishment, they were keen upholders of centralized authority represented by the capital. Yet, by their time, the literary hegemony of London was not absolute. 'By seeing London, I have seen as much of life as the world can shew', Dr Johnson remarked to Boswell, but, in fiction in particular, characters were often bored by and fearful of the London he valued.[3]

Sentimentalism was always rather at odds with the capital. With its emphasis on community, it found distressing the anonymity and possible viciousness of the large city. In mid-century literature, London was frequently the place of vice and frivolous pleasure; in later decades it stood also for social malice and economic greed. The average sentimental novel opposing vice and virtue took the virtuous hero to the horrors of London; it then allowed him to escape into the rural provinces to find a happy ending.

In the country it seemed that man and virtue had not yet parted company. In his *Discourse on the Origins of Inequality among Men* (1755), Rousseau found decadence in the large cities of civilization and turned instead to nature for purity. The country became a literary fashion, a state where mind harmonized with natural beauty and nature displayed human moods.

Although far fewer writers than literary characters came from distant picturesque parts, Wales or Northumbria for example, a considerable number, especially women, did come from the more substantial provincial towns. Towards the end of the century in Ipswich, Norwich, Bath, Lichfield and Bristol there were clusters of readers and writers of novels, poetry and advice books. Such provincials were very frequently the correspondents of the London magazines and the writers of their occasional poetry. Some authors combined their actual location with the literary image of rural retreat: Sterne, for example, wrote his dedication to *Tristram Shandy* in 'a bye corner of this kingdom . . . in a retired thatch'd house'.

The interest in the countryside brought with it an enthusiasm for landscape gardening which paralleled literary fashion: 'Poetry, Painting, and Gardening, or the Science of Landscape will forever by men of taste be deemed Three Sisters, or the *Three New Graces* who dress and adorn nature,' wrote Horace Walpole.[4] In the first half of the century, following the theories of Stephen Switzer in *Ichnographia Rustica* (1718) and the practice of William Kent, taste moved from continental formality to the emblematic garden, like Kent's learned, classical example at Stowe, full of poetic and patriotic inscriptions and meaningful statues. Such gardening was little appreciated by poets of sensibility – Joseph Warton and Thomas Gray for example – who wanted a more expressive landscape and rejected the paraphernalia of bowling greens, ditches and shell-grottoes, to use Gray's contemptuous words. Landscapes, both created and discovered, were influenced by the paintings of Claude Lorrain and Salvator Rosa (the inspiration also of the literary sentimental scenes of Ann Radcliffe); they should be expressive and affective, not in the bland monotonous way detractors associated with Lancelot (Capability) Brown's designs, but in a stimulating fashion that varied the moods of the observer and taught emotional reaction. Thomas Whateley's *Observations on Modern Gardening* (1770) stressed strong spontaneous feeling and limited the intricate intellectual response Kent required.

The family

The eighteenth-century family is a much disputed entity. Some historians, most notably Lawrence Stone in *The Family, Sex and Marriage 1500–1800* (1977), declare that the falling death rate of infants infused sentiment into the business of childbearing and raising. At the same time decline in the importance of extended kinship ties and increase in the power of the state encouraged the strengthening of the patriarchal nuclear family with its affective bonds. Others such as Peter Laslett and E. A. Wrigley dispute this thesis. In *Population and History* (1969) Wrigley suggests that the inflationist economy of the later eighteenth century made the economic unit of the nuclear family even more insecure than formerly, while Peter Laslett in *The World We Have Lost* (1965) and *Family Life and Illicit Love in Earlier Generations* (1977) sees the family tottering under the economic and social movements of the times. Whatever the historical truth of the matter, some change in the expression of attitudes to the family certainly did occur, and an emphasis unknown before was placed by literature and art on the image of the small, loving nuclear family and on the kindly parent. At a time when the loose financial ties of early capitalism were emerging in the market-place, sentimentalism expressed a longing not only for a domestic close-knit family but for a community firmly linked by sentiment and familial structures.

As with the eighteenth-century family, there is disagreement among historians over the interpretation of marriage. H. J. Habakkuk argued that, to maintain and increase landed wealth which at this time signified power, marriage at least in the upper and upper-middle classes became more than ever an economic transaction.[5] Stone, however, seeing a growth of affective ties amongst the upper-middle class and the squirearchy, considers that marriages were increasingly entered into with the expectation of affection and companionship and with the intention of carefully raising children.

As in the case of the family, the only certainty is that, in Christopher Hill's words, *'talk about* marriage for love increased'.[6] This talk was loud and prolonged. Numerous authors lamented the miseries of unbreakable matrimony, its financial liabilities for men, its oppressiveness for women, and its possible destruction of happiness for both. Yet, simultaneously, the married state and women's role within it were exalted, to a high point where economic and political aspects were entirely blurred.

Women

The changes in class and family connect with the change in the position of women. Many female writers felt that their sex had lost ground economically. Men were thought to be intruding into women's home occupations such as millinery, and the house was no longer seen as the workplace. A battle over childbirth was joined which ended in the triumph of men and their forceps, and female midwifery gave place to male obstetrics, at least in the higher orders. For the first time in English history the middle-class family seemed to need only the work of the man. Foreigners marvelled at the idleness thrust on English women, whose business was little more than coquetry in youth and motherhood or fashion in later years. In this situation husbands grew more expensive and the jointure (money paid to a woman in widowhood) was lowered in relation to the dowry she brought into the marriage. Women became commodities more than helpmates or independent economic actors.

Supporting the domestic private status of women was the double sexual standard. Always to some extent present in western culture, it was blatantly reiterated in the eighteenth century. Throughout much of the previous century, chastity as a meaningful Christian state was enjoined on men as well as women in conduct books. But, as early as 1678, Lord Halifax could find criminal in women what was mere error in men. In the eighteenth century sexual continence became a predominantly female virtue.

In literature virginity and chastity for women kept something of their Christian aura, but in life they seem to have become rather more practical and politically motivated. Virginity as a long-standing state, not simply a necessary enhancement of the young girl, was deprived of its religious significance and downgraded; the older virgin sank into the old maid, a figure to be mocked and abused.

The family was the place of value and activity for the chaste woman, but her position within it was problematic. Primogeniture had shored up the power of the eldest son, for, as H. J. Habakkuk has argued, changes in inheritance patterns, whereby property was more and more concentrated in the eldest son, meant a downgrading of the father in relation to his son; nothing, however, mitigated the daughter's absolute dependence on her father. In the ordinary course of things, this dependence would be expected to give way to a new one, on a husband. But towards the close of the eighteenth century, improvements in hygiene and living standards increased the hardier female population disproportionately, so that it grew to contain a greater number of spinsters. In the middle and upper classes these unattached women had little opportunity for activity beyond the family and they could only hold to the daughterly role or imitate the wife as nurse, governess or companion. In sentimental literature the father–daughter tie would be shorn of its social and economic problems and be marvellously extolled.

In *Sir Charles Grandison* Richardson noted both the 'unprovided and helpless' state of single women of 'slender fortune . . . when family-connexions are dissolved' and the contempt directed towards working women. Echoing other early eighteenth-century writers such as Mary Astell and Lady Mary Wortley Montagu, he recommended 'Protestant Nunneries' in which single women of small or no fortune might live in freedom but 'under such regulations as it would be a disgrace for a modest or good woman not to comply with'.[7] Nothing, however, was established, and unprotected genteel women remained largely superfluous.

If women had far less power in society than men, they grew great in moral importance. In *The Country and the City* (1973), Raymond Williams has described the increasing separation of traditional virtues from economic life in the eighteenth century. While men pursued the practical business of commerce, women became preservers of the religious values of charity and compassion. Instead of being Eves as in former times, symbols of sexuality and opacity through their crucial part in the myth of the Fall, they grew into Protestant virgins, the consciences of society. To sweeten and enforce their uncomfortable role as moral guardians, a coy sort of gallantry developed. Women became almost invariably the 'fair sex', and open misogyny of the urbane Restoration kind was rare. A furore greeted the publication of the cynical letters of the Earl of Chesterfield, who considered women simply children of a larger growth and suggested their use in the sexual education of well-born young men.

The chaste woman became not only the preserver of moral values but also, especially in drama and fiction, a kind of token of male honour for the commercial classes. Rank was absolute only for the aristocrat, who must duel and die to support it, but in the market-place economic status was not final like birth, and social violence for honour seemed to need a new place of justification.

The chaste female body appeared, then, a private family commodity for which the man could reasonably fight or go to law, as Richardson's novels and numerous legal cases testify.

The female body also became an organism peculiarly susceptible to influence. Women were thought to express emotions with their bodies more sincerely and spontaneously than men; hence their propensity to crying, blushing and fainting. At the same time, such a susceptible organism could easily become erratic and deranged. So hysteria, an especially female disease, became prominent in eighteenth-century England – just as melancholia or hypochondria grew common in sensitive men – and formed the subject of numerous treatises, notably by Robert James (*Medical Dictionary*, 1743) and George Cheyne (*English Malady*, 1733). Still connected with the womb – although the old idea of the womb's wandering was no longer credited – hysteria was thought to result from great internal heat, often linked with a woman's controlled amorous inclinations; it was not a fall from human to animal nature like some forms of mania but an exaggeration of very human susceptibility or physical sensibility. As Michel Foucault describes it:

> The entire female body is riddled by obscure but strangely direct paths of sympathy . . . from one extremity of its organic space to the other, it encloses a perpetual possibility of hysteria. The sympathetic sensibility of her organism . . . condemns woman to . . . diseases of the nerves.[8]

The new sentimental and susceptible woman was partially constructed in the early eighteenth century in the influential pages of the *Tatler* and the *Spectator*, associated with Joseph Addison and Richard Steele. In both periodicals, sentimental virtues of benevolence and compassion gained ascendancy over the courtly values of wit and sophistication. Pity, Steele declared, was 'the Weakness' of his heart and in his writings he presented pathetic images to teach a proper tearful response. Against the harsh, knowing ethics of the Restoration, he exalted domesticity and gentleness, and he urged love and common sense in marriage over wit and spiritedness in courtship. Great men were seen in domestic scenes gently playing with children, and the tyrannical patriarch was made both socially disastrous and ridiculous.

Yet, while Addison and Steele opposed the tyranny of ill-natured, aggressive men and noted the cruelty of the old morality to women, they did not question the social order that allowed such tyranny. In fact they wanted a sentimental version of the patriarchal order, not its abolition. So, in place of the extrafamilial sexual woman or the bitter virago of courtly Restoration literature, they urged the gentle feeling lady, entirely familial and entirely subordinate, while domesticity was elevated to the female equivalent of a male profession. Addison wanted women to be tender and intelligent mothers and faithful wives; in the *Spectator* he claimed that he would lead them 'through all the becoming Duties of Virginity, Marriage, and Widowhood'.

In the articles of Addison and Steele virtues took on specific genders: 'There is a Sort of Sex in Souls' and 'The Virtues have respectively a Masculine and Feminine Cast.' To support and justify the new exalted subordination of women, the *Tatler* and the *Spectator* stressed the special female association with sensibility, giving inferior women a superiority in their contingency and service: 'Women were formed to temper Mankind, and sooth them into Tenderness and Compassion.' Female virtues were superior ones, then, but they were to be deployed for the benefit of men who could function pretty well without them.[9]

To many, the sentimental emphasis illustrated in the female constructions of Addison and Steele seemed an obvious advance on the harsh raillery of the Restoration and Augustan periods. It gave centrality to women – albeit strangely constructed ones – and brought female consciousness under investigation; there is nothing in earlier literature to set against the probings of *Pamela, Clarissa* or *La Nouvelle Héloïse.* Yet many men and women also felt ambivalent about the construction, seeing its possible implications. Certainly it could be variously interpreted as Rousseau, probably its most influential proponent, indicates. His works loudly assert the sentimental gender distinction, a biological absolute that separates female from male physically, mentally and emotionally. In one formulation the female qualities posited are highly valued and they must act on male society to make all form an orderly, harmonious community. In another, however, they are to be feared and avoided by men; male dominance is enjoined and women are regarded as simply contingent beings whose qualities, if allowed influence, would emasculate, cripple and effeminately socialize men.

The pious passivity which women's idealization seems to demand in them appears much at odds with their energy in one area of activity: literary enterprise. In the eighteenth century women entered the market-place as consumers: middle- and upper-class women attended theatres and bought plays, poems and pamphlets; women of all except the lowest classes read novels, tales and tracts. They entered too as producers, Amazons of the pen, as Dr Johnson termed them, and by many they were even felt to dominate the fiction market.

In the presentation of themselves as producers, women were influenced by the current images of passive virtue and, after a false and naughty start in the Restoration, they reliably learned to depict themselves as helpless ladies, moral monitors and chaste entertainers. Whatever their pose, however, they provoked some uneasiness in male authors and critics who sometimes exaggerated their numbers and sometimes foretold their total dominance – and so debasement – of literature. Occasionally male critics were moved to declare men's actual mastery in most ungallant terms: 'Women we have often eagerly placed near the throne of literature; if they seize it, forgetful of our fondness, we can turn them from it.'[10]

Religion

The seventeenth century was shadowed by the Civil War and doctrinal and sectarian quarrels. After the Restoration, the appetite for bitter religious polemic decreased, although disputes over doctrine certainly continued – as the intolerant outbursts in Fielding's *Joseph Andrews* suggest. Several groups and sects, however, moved away from theological speculation to emphasize human conduct and morality. They avoided stress on the orthodox view of original sin and expressed a hope in human goodness and perfectibility, so important for sentimentalism. Philosophically the most significant of these sects is the Cambridge Platonists, a loose association of Anglican moralists mostly of Puritan descent, but affected by Plato and Plotinus in their mystical apprehension of the order of things.

Perhaps the most immediate influence on the Platonists was adversarial: Thomas Hobbes, a seventeenth-century writer who, for Platonists and later sentimentalists alike, expressed the cautionary materialist alternative to belief in human goodness. Refuting Hobbes became the convenient starting-point of many sentimental and Christian philosophers.

In *Leviathan* (1651), Hobbes proposed a kind of secular Calvinism, seeing human nature as in the main irredeemably fallen, and the spring of human action as egoism and desire for power. People were material entities who acted through necessity; the natural man was necessarily and simply selfish and greedy: 'I put for a generall inclination of all mankind, a perpetuall and restless desire of Power after power, that ceaseth only in Death.'[11] Virtue became relative, another form of egoism, and community a herding together of the weak out of fear of the strong. For the eighteenth century these propositions were stated in modified form by Bernard de Mandeville in *The Fable of the Bees* (1714–28), in which he wittily argued that the impulse to apparently virtuous action was in fact selfish interest.

The Cambridge Platonists aimed to counter Hobbes's doctrine of necessity, as well as Calvin's one of predestination, and refute his mechanistic account of humanity. They argued that man did have freedom of will and that ethics were not relative but eternal. Several posited an innate faculty of morality, although giving different accounts of its genesis, and all felt that moral principles were self-evident, that moral consciousness existed outside religious revelation. There was a godlikeness in humanity, a perfectibility, albeit in a millenarian theological context, and the human mind was actively able to corrrespond with an assumed universal harmony. With so optimistic a view, most of the Platonists supported liberty of conscience and they saw community as a fulfilment of humanity, not a huddling together through fear.[12]

The Cambridge Platonists in turn influenced a later generation of Anglican thinkers, the Latitudinarians, who continued to see Christianity as a moral system based on the concept of innate virtue, and who stressed charity as the supreme quality and proper manifestation of Christian faith. The ultimate direction of both groups and of established Dissenting sects was towards a broader and broader interpretation of theology, in fact towards an intellectual belief in reason and nature that almost denied the need for Christian revelation.

In this rationalist climate, many people, especially those from the less educated classes, felt the absence of enthusiastic and spiritual faith; to this absence the Evangelical movements, including Wesleyan Methodism in England and the Great Awakening in America, were a response. Impressed by the Cambridge Platonists and their emphasis on benevolence and humility over dogma, the Wesley brothers and George Whitefield likewise wanted 'Christ formed in our hearts' and a life lived in Christian community. But they also wanted the element of enthusiastic faith and emotional drama that would appeal to the mass of the people. Their parish was often in the provinces, among the lower classes and away from the universities. Meetings were the opposite of formal church-going, emotional spectacles demanding in the open air the kind of response that sentimental literature wanted in the closet. The hymns of Methodism, like Charles Wesley's 'Jesu, Lover of my Soul', are a kind of sentimental dramatic poetry reaching out to the singers and taking them into the religious theatre. Like sentimental fiction and drama, they teach and provoke emotion.

With its emphasis on the loving kindness of Jesus and the charity of the individual heart, the emotional Christianity of Methodism fed the sentimental concern for the victim and the dispossessed. The humanitarian movement was couched in religious terminology, and its various causes were prosecuted with crusading zeal. These humanitarian concerns also produced an immense quantity of literature, and slavery in particular became a fine subject for treatment. As the dramatist Richard Cumberland unkindly expressed it, the slave was 'fair game' for poets, an absolute 'mine of sentiment'.

Philosophy

For Isaac Newton, caught in the optimism of the Cambridge Platonists, external nature was a wonderful spectacle, whose operation was to be studied, admired and understood. As his mechanical construction of the universe controlled by rational laws became largely accepted in the first half of the eighteenth century, ethics and aesthetics no longer seemed to require heaven as necessary validation. Nature itself, first the vastness of space and then the sublimity of earth, became an expression of God through which finite people could approach the infinite and understand both beauty and morality. Natural laws declared God's beneficence, and in the *Principia Mathematica* (1687) order and harmony were proved universal principles; from them ethics and aesthetics could to some extent be deduced, although many contemporaries regretted Newton's own hesitation at drawing ethical conclusions.

The external world was processed through humanity, not initially through intellectual effort but through sensation and feeling. Body and mind were connected, and sight in particular formed the basis of intellectual and imaginative constructs. For eighteenth-century ideas of sensibility, deriving in part from the empirical science of Newton, the most important figure is John Locke. Although his primary concern was the philosophy of knowledge, his major popular influence came through his ideas on psychology, especially his notions of the mind as a blank sheet and of ideas originating in sensation and connecting through association.

Locke tried to give mathematical certainty to knowledge and morality. He argued that, despite the fact that moral ideas derived from sense experience, relations among these ideas were fixed, so that morality was capable of demonstration as well as mathematics – although he notably stopped short of demonstrating it. Influenced by the Cambridge Platonists in seeing the good as that which causes pleasure and diminishes pain, Locke none the less totally opposed their belief in innate principles. Knowledge and morality were not given, but were rather the result of human activity: 'God has furnished men with faculties sufficient to direct them in the way they should take if they will but seriously employ them that way.'[13]

In the *Essay Concerning Human Understanding* (1690), Locke was concerned with the logical content of the mind, but, in passing, he investigated introspection as well, bringing into focus the mind's subjectivity, its reflection on itself. He noted the momentary nature of apprehension and mood and the chance construction of associations that seemed to have no logical justification. To later sentimentalists he taught the evanescence and primacy of impulse and suggested that sensibility – openness through sensation to the world – was the only route to knowledge.

Locke's pupil, the second Earl of Shaftesbury, is often considered the founder of, or the prime influence on, sentimental philosophy of the moral sense school. His rhapsodical writings, collected in 1711 as *Characteristics*, came to inhabit the minds of many people who had grown dubious about some orthodox Christian doctrines but who remained unhappy at Locke's materialism. Shaftesbury's liberating secular humanism was immensely influential in the first part of the century, but declined from fashion in the last; by that time his ideas were commonplace in the culture.

To the diverse and varied universe of Newton, Shaftesbury responded with enthusiasm, seeing in the great aspects of nature the shadow of divinity. From Locke he learned to understand the external world through looking at the mind at work and to connect natural appearances and human sensations. Like his mentor, Shaftesbury seemed to be struggling for a vocabulary to describe a new sense of human psychology, of the mind as open to sensation and continually changing in response, and of identity as formed from the fleeting moments of consciousness. Psychological processes became dramas of the mind, a fascinating theatre to the self-conscious.

Shaftesbury differed from Locke in wishing to see the openness of sensibility welded to benevolence, in this early period a 'manly' attribute opposing 'womanish' self-interest and fear. He strongly disagreed with his old tutor over the notion of innate ideas and he saw the doctrine of the blank sheet or *tabula rasa* as materialist and dangerous. In a letter of 1716, he claimed that with this doctrine Locke 'struck at all fundamentals, threw all Order and Virtue out of the World, and made the very Ideas of these (which are the same as those of God) *unnatural*'.[14]

Like the Cambridge Platonists, who greatly influenced his thinking, Shaftesbury posited a moral sense, near reason but also close to intuition. This inborn conscience is the source of moral distinctions and heads humanity towards benevolence and friendliness, away from the egoism and self-interest of Hobbes and Mandeville. God appears the best-natured being possible, a gentleman on a grand scale; the world becomes his work of art continuously created: 'everything is govern'd, order'd, or regulated *for the best*, by a designing Principle, or Mind, necessarily good and permanent.'

Shaftesbury achieved an extraordinary aestheticizing of morality, so that in his writings the good and virtuous became synonymous with the beautiful. To philosophize was 'to learn what is *just* in Society, and *beautiful* in Nature, and the Order of the World'; to be good was to see the beauty of virtue:

No sooner are actions viewed, no sooner the human affections and passions discerned (and they are most of them as soon discerned as felt) than straight an inward eye distinguishes and sees the fair and shapely, the amiable and admirable, apart from the deform'd, the foul, the odious or the despicable. How is it possible therefore not to own that as these distinctions have their foundation in nature, the discernment itself is natural and from nature alone.

The main end of his work, Shaftesbury declared, was 'to assert the Reality of a Beauty and Charm in *moral* as well as natural Subjects'. Virtue was enjoyable as a spectacle in the self and in others. It needed no divine rewards and punishment as its support.[15]

Shaftesbury's thought is developed and modified by many subsequent 'moral' philosophers, especially the Scottish Francis Hutcheson, David Hume and Adam Smith, all more bourgeois, anti-establishment and initially more culturally marginal than their aristocratic predecessor. Hutcheson moved Shaftesbury's philosophy towards the utilitarianism always inherent in it and propounded the idea later popularized by Jeremy Bentham: '*That action is best*, which procures the *greatest* Happiness for the *greatest* Number.' The title of one of Hutcheson's works indicates his acceptance of Shaftesbury's association of aesthetics and ethics: *An Enquiry into the Origin of Our Ideas of Beauty and Virtue* (1725). Moral sense is postulated and good actions become their own reward. But Hutcheson goes beyond Shaftesbury in emphasizing benevolence as the whole of virtue in human affairs.

Beginning under the influence of Hutcheson, David Hume moved closer to Shaftesbury in accepting benevolence as merely one affection among others; if it were the only virtue, he argued, it would become strictly utilitarian – the good would be defined as anything leading to the greater happiness of many. Benevolence derives less from Christian humility, often its source in later eighteenth-century fiction, than from pride which is selfish in origin, but which none the less nudges a person towards social virtue. The limitations of benevolence for Hume become clearest when he discusses justice. In his understanding of this concept, he shows himself a synthesizer of philosophies, believing in social virtues with Shaftesbury but veering towards Hobbes in his view of justice as an artificial creation, constructed by reason and founded on self-interest.

With both Hutcheson and Shaftesbury, however, Hume rejects the ethics of rationalism, and he goes further than either in insisting on the impotence of reason as the instrument of moral restraint. It is passion that moves us to act, he asserts: 'Morality . . . is more properly felt than judged of . . . To have a sense of virtue is nothing but to feel satisfaction of a particular kind.'

Like Shaftesbury and unlike Hobbes, Locke and Mandeville, Hume found community natural, based on the herding instinct and the human desire for fellowship: 'It appears that a tendency to public good, and to the promoting of peace, harmony, and order in society does always, by affecting the benevolent principles of our frame, engage us on the side of social virtues.'[16] Although Hume later moved from this optimistic assertion, in his *Treatise of Human Nature* (1740) he makes community a spontaneous formation, a combination of self and other through sympathy and tenderness that elide individual differences. Sympathy, the inclination 'to sympathize with others, and to receive by communication their inclinations and sentiments' is the basis of social harmony. In contemporary medical treatises it acts similarly within the body, allowing organs to communicate with each other and to react and suffer together.

Like his friend Hume, Adam Smith noted the power of sympathy, but he saw it less as a spontaneous than as a contrived mode. In *The Theory of Moral Sentiments* (1759), he investigated the means by which moral judgements are formed. Stressing the specular nature of sympathy, he argued that it derives from an imaginary spectator within, who allows us to change places with a sufferer and put his or her interests before our own; hence we act benevolently. This imaginary changing of place makes sympathy less optimistic than in Hume's construction, for it becomes not an original spontaneous feeling but more of a moral duty. In addition it can be deplorable as well as good. The sympathetic, loving ties of the family are admirable, but the reverence of the poor for the rich, although it might order society, is none the less corrupting. As the pupil of Hutcheson, Adam Smith accepted the importance of benevolence as a virtue, but he denied a special moral sense. His ideal man has benevolence flanked by the unsentimental attributes of prudence and self-command.

The instability obvious in Adam Smith's *Theory of Moral Sentiments* makes it a fitting end to a line of British moral philosophy. It is the last major work of the period to admit the sentimental aim of trying systematically to link morality and emotion, an attempt not seen again until it was made pejoratively by A. J. Ayer this century. After the *Theory*, philosophical energy passed into the reforming rationalism of, for example, the Dissenter Richard Price and the radical anarchist William Godwin, and later into utilitarianism, which separated the happiness principle of sentimental thought from benevolence and virtue. Two decades after publishing *The Theory of Moral Sentiments*, Adam Smith went on to write the far more influential work, *The Wealth of Nations*, in which he seems to echo Hobbes rather than Shaftesbury: 'It is not from the benevolence of the butcher, the brewer, or the baker, that we expect our dinner, but from their regard to their own interest.'[17]

By the late eighteenth century, the ideas of the British moral philosophers had been largely assimilated or rejected, and Rousseau had become the dominant name in popular sentimental thought. Rousseau took as the centre of interest the subjectivity which Locke and Shaftesbury had probed, and sensibility as special and refined susceptibility became a source of authority to which traditional morality had to bow. In *La Nouvelle Héloïse* (1761), Rousseau even condoned his heroine's sexual activity outside marriage, since his focus was on her superior sensibility. This focus attracted many female writers, especially towards the end of the century, although most, like Mary Wollstonecraft and Mary Hays, feared the anarchic stress on overwhelming feeling and the linking of sex and sensibility. Male authors had no such anxiety, and the idea of free love based on spontaneous emotion had a vogue in the 1780s and 1790s in, for example, Payne Knight's *Essay on the Worship of Priapus* (1786) and Blake's *Visions of the Daughters of Albion* (1793).

Rousseau agreed with Shaftesbury in seeing humanity as innately good, as having naturally an impulse to pity and to help suffering. In the 'Profession of faith of a Savoyard vicar' in *Emile* (1762), acts of conscience are declared to be sentiments, not judgements. But human hearts have become overlaid by the evils of social and political institutions, hence the apparent viciousness of people. So Rousseau stressed the need for intellectual and emotional freedom in order that morality might flourish. By so doing he insisted on a political dimension that made it possible for anti-sentimentalists later to blame both sentiment and Rousseau for the evils of anarchy and revolutionary France.

Critical ideas

Much influenced by Isaac Newton in his apprehension of great nature, the critic John Dennis was an important formulator of sentimental aesthetics. He was harshly ridiculed by Pope in *The Dunciad*, especially in the notes where his opinions are portrayed as rhapsodical and mad. Instead of evaluating literature morally and aesthetically in the manner of Dryden, Pope or, later, Johnson,

Dennis described the psychological processes of literary creation and consumption, finding the basis of both in passion.

The sublime became his concern. He knew Longinus's treatise intimately, but he considered the sublime less as a rhetorical practice in the manner of Longinus than as a psychological effect. For Dennis, the source of sublimity was ultimately God, manifesting his power through a nature of vastness – volcanoes, earthquakes, lions and wars. In *The Advancement and Reformation of Modern Poetry* (1701) and *The Grounds of Criticism in Poetry* (1704) he analysed – and exalted – his own emotional experience and enthusiastic response to the naturally powerful. Poetry, like nature, moved people by exciting passion. Great poetry provoked great passions, especially the enthusiastic ones of admiration, terror, horror and joy. The proper response to art, as to stupendous nature, was 'delightful Horrour' and 'terrible Joy'.

In his reactive rhapsody Dennis did not lose sight of the instructive aim of art. He declared that art should never run 'counter to moral virtue' and, whatever its subject and genre, its purpose should always be the reformation or improvement of manners. But, since art was in its essence emotional, it would fulfil its aim not by intellectual persuasiveness but by its affective power.

The emphasis, clear in Dennis's writings, on emotional response rather than rational judgement marks the sentimental critic throughout the eighteenth century. It was, however, still a novelty in 1712 when Joseph Addison contributed his essays, 'The pleasures of the imagination', to the *Spectator*. In these he again explained the production and consumption of literature in terms of feeling, considering, for example, that the effect of tragedy derived from the spectators' fear for themselves. He connected the excitement of the reaction to external nature with the excitement of creativity and literary response; the sense of the great in nature, a God–given faculty acting in humanity especially through sight, was associated with the imagination that produced and responded to poetry.

Addison popularized the idea of the sublime as emotionally stimulating. Literature expressing earthly sublimity could provoke a similar response to that aroused by gigantic nature – as exemplified by Milton's *Paradise Lost*, which became pre-eminently the poem of the sublime. In the 1740s and 1750s works on the sublime as a psychological stimulus and response proliferated: from John Baillie, Joseph Spence, William Hogarth and Robert Lowth. The most influential was, however, Edmund Burke's *Philosophical*

Enquiry into the Origin of our Ideas of the Sublime and Beautiful (1757, revised and enlarged in 1759).

In his work Burke once more stressed the affective nature of literature, and he began his study of sublimity and beauty not by a description of the literary devices used to obtain them but by an investigation of human psychology: 'We yield to sympathy, what we refuse to description.' The aim of literature is 'to affect rather by sympathy than imitation; to display rather the effect of things on the mind of the speaker, or of others, than to present a clear idea of the things themselves.'[18] Here works of art do not necessarily contain an intellectual meaning; instead they primarily provoke the reader's participation in a mood. We respond to the description of response as much as to the portrayal of action. It is a lesson taken to heart by writers of sentimental fiction.

Remembering the connection of mind and body stressed by Locke, other critics became more intimate about the physiological nature of aesthetic response. In *Essay on Taste* (1755) John Gilbert Cooper, for example, noted that the proper reader stance before the work of art is an 'instantaneous glow of Pleasure which thrills throu' our whole Frame and Seizes upon the Applause of the Heart before the intellectual Power Reason can descend from the Throne of the Mind to ratify its Approbation'.[19] In another *Essay on Taste* four years later, Alexander Gerard predicated taste on sensibility: to respond to literature, readers must be susceptible and easily moved, so that they may catch the nuances of passion and pathos. In Lord Kames's *Elements of Criticism* (1762), the reader's experience becomes a rhapsody, 'a kind of reverie' where 'the consciousness of self, and of reading' disappears.[20]

In Germany, sentimental ideas of reader response were systematized and investigated with more rigour than in England. Lessing, for example, in *The Hamburg Dramaturgy* (1767–8) united Aristotle's notions of pity and fear by regarding the tragic effect as fear for ourselves, in the manner of Addison, and pity for others. The effect of tragedy became not so much cathartic, purging emotions so that spectators might continue about their daily business, as educative, refining the capacities of the audience to feel. A work of art reached out into life and changed pity into virtue.

Like poetry, the idea of the poet caused sentimental critics to grow rhapsodical. Severed from long apprenticeship to rules and styles, the artist became mystified into a superior sensibility, a kind of emotional vibrator. Dennis saw his greatness in his capacity to feel enthusiastic passion and in his emotional distinction from others; Shaftesbury considered him as imitating in his art the divine act of creation itself. In time the poet became bardic, magical, animated in William Duff's phrase 'with a kind of divine fury'. Shakespeare was the main exemplar: in Joseph Warton's 'The Enthusiast' (1744–8) he is directly inspired by nature as a babe and the location of his inspiration is 'the sacred place' to be contemplated with 'religious awe'. Opposing Dr Johnson's *Lives of the English Poets* (1781), which argued that poets should be judged as morally accountable men and that critics required application and patience, Percival Stockdale in *Lectures on the Truly Eminent English Poets* (1807) insisted that poetic geniuses were outside the ordinary rules of human conduct and could not be judged as others. A proper response to poetry was not comparison and criticism but wonder and complete surrender.

III *Drama*

The stage was the main early battle ground of sentimentalism, with the opposing side represented by the witty, urbane and intellectual drama of the late Restoration. Immediately after his arrival in England, Charles II authorized two patent theatres which, under his patronage, would serve the court. The fare was mainly revamped plays from the classical and Jacobean periods, but new works were welcome, especially those in the high heroic and tragic mode and in a comic style amalgamating Ben Jonson and classical French comedy. It was the comic mode that came to cause offence since, despite its traditional origins, it differed markedly in morality from its models.

Overtly concerned with sex, gender conflicts and money, Restoration comedy gave a new prestige to cleverness and hedonism, allowing respect to slip from the chaste and virtuous to the sophisticated and libidinous. Men who cleverly planned seduction and women who wittily railed against men were exalted, and the losers were not so much the morally bad as the stupid, the naïve and the emotionally self-indulgent.

Towards the end of the century, many factors caused a reaction against the aristocratic mode of Restoration drama. The political crises concerning James II made its sophistication seem frivolous. Audiences grew increasingly heterogeneous and included a large proportion of people from the middle class who had no sympathy with its style. Women, whose earlier presence in the theatre had seemed to many an indicator of the decadence of the age, became more prominent as spectators, but now they appeared to signify a need for proper restraint on drama. Several playwrights including Colley Cibber declared their works especially suitable for 'the Ladies' or pleasing to 'the Fair Sex', who wanted plays in which in Swift's mocking words, 'their sex is deified and adored'. Theatrical quarrels and a growth in the number of playhouses caused rivalry for the new audience of mixed classes and genders, and a drama different from the intellectual aristocratic comedy encouraged by Charles II seemed increasingly desirable.

Jeremy Collier, a clergyman, reflects the changing temper of the times. In 1698 he aimed a blast at the courtly Restoration theatre which made its 'top characters libertines, and [gave] them success in their debauchery'. *A Short View of the Immorality, and Profaneness of the English Stage* was an answer directed in particular at Wycherley and Vanbrugh whose *The Provok'd Wife* dresses a man as a parson and lets him whore, drink and profane. Collier complained that Restoration comedy had debauched the age and that it exhibited 'smuttiness of expression', swearing, libertinage and lewdness. In its place he demanded simplicity of morality: 'As good and evil are different in themselves, so they ought to be differently mark'd.' He opens his introduction uncompromisingly: 'The business of plays is to recommend virtue, and discountenance vice.'[1]

Vanbrugh answered Collier by affirming that comedy taught people how they should act by showing them how they actually did, while Congreve took issue with the narrowness of Collier's implied view of art. Although the controversy raged until at least the 1720s, the future was with the clergyman; as Dr Johnson noted: 'Comedy grew more modest, and Collier lived to see the reward of his labour in the reformation of the theatre.'[2]

Sentimental drama which developed during the late seventeenth and early eighteenth centuries, and flourished throughout the rest of the eighteenth century, severed the tie of court and stage. It is associated with the parliamentarians, the supporters of the Protestant succession, the mercantile and less educated classes, with women, and those who held Whiggish sympathies. It was therefore deplored by the major Tory satirists, Swift and Pope, and it is not accidental that the arch butt of *The Dunciad* is the sentimental dramatist Colley Cibber.

By mid–century the theatre had registered many changes from the Restoration. Audiences had become less riotous and play-wrights could expect a measure of decorous behaviour. By modern standards spectators were still rowdy, however, and there was much complaint by theatre people about inattention and the use of the pit for purposes other than playwatching. In physical appear-ance too there were alterations. The main theatres were growing larger, and the stage was becoming more clearly separated from the audience, a process which culminated in Garrick's banishing of spectators from the stage altogether.

Acting was also modified. A kind of performing associated with Garrick suited sentimental theories, for, where the older style had concentrated on technique and declamation, the newer emphasized communication of emotion. At the beginning of the century Le Brun's influential *Expressions des passions* was translated into English; it advanced the notion that every idea had an exact corresponding expression. A language of expression and gesture was elaborated in such works as Aaron Hill's *Essay on the Art of Acting* (1753) which insisted that the idea should be impressed on the body as well as the face. Hill felt that sensibility was the source of genuine acting and he was enthusiastic over Garrick's method which stressed the feeling performance and the expression of attitude in all parts of the body. In a letter to Garrick in 1749 he praised the actor for bringing 'the passions, first, into your eye, before you *spoke* a syllable'. Richard Cumberland in his *Memoirs* paid a similar tribute by declaring Garrick 'alive in every muscle and in every feature'.[3]

In Garrick's expressive method, the emphasis was on character as attitude, on the individual scene rather than on the play as a totality, and on gesture rather than flow of speech. Consequently the emotional tableau, so common in sentimental writing generally, predominated over narrative coherence, a tendency supported by the fashion of the time for paintings of actors in high dramatic and static moments: as Aaron Hill expressed it in *The Prompter*, 'Upon occasion of some striking scene, we should, as in a finished history-piece, the work of a great master, behold the stage *one living group* of figures' (May 1735).

In France, Diderot too promoted the idea of the tableau in his plea for serious bourgeois drama which would deliver moral lessons to spectators and move them to goodness. At high moments, the scene might resemble a canvas of the artist Greuze, who gained great popularity in France in the 1760s with his emotional paintings of domestic life, of a father cursing, a mother serving her family, or a young girl crying over a dead bird.

The change in size and arrangement of the theatre meant less intimacy in the drama, and, before microphones and electric lights, the grand gesture was essential if the actor was to communicate to distant spectators. Spectacle flourished and some traditional plays like Shakespeare's were stripped of their subtlety so that their potential for pageant could be exploited. Pantomimes and comic operas shared the stage with displays of jugglers, acrobats and wild animals.

In the early eighteenth century the number of London theatres grew, but the Licensing Act of 1737 reduced them again to two and brought plays under the censorship of the Lord Chamberlain. A shock was given to satirical drama and playwrights like Henry Fielding gave up the theatre for the novel.

Yet, with the focus on the actual dramatic fare in the theatre, none of these changes in audience, in numbers and arrangement of playhouses, in style of acting and in the content of plays, should be exaggerated. Political drama, for example, sometimes said to have been killed by the Licensing Act, flourished throughout the eighteenth century, although after the Act specific personal abuse became more dangerous. Provincial theatres, beginning in the early decades, burgeoned in the later, accompanied at the end of the century by the rage for private theatrical houses. Spectacle had been a part of certain modes of drama in all ages. Above all, the plays most performed and watched remained the same, although they were much rewritten to suit the demands of the new audience.

Throughout the century playwrights refocused and cleaned up older plays to make them into more suitable vehicles of sentiment and theatrical gesture. Ribaldry and bawdry were removed from Shakespeare and other Renaissance dramatists, and classical comedy was chastened; Restoration plays were rehabilitated as sentimental drama. Plots were transformed so that the comic became the moral and the tragic became the pathetic; the centre of the stage was held less by active heroes than by passive and suffering female victims.

Robert Dodsley was one remodeller; he fashioned a white

version of *Othello* which demanded audience sympathy less for the faulty male than for female virtue in distress. William Whitehead remade Corneille's *Horace* with Horatia as the primary character. Wycherley's *The Country Wife*, in Garrick's version of 1766, avoided adultery and made money inessential. Some plays went through multiple transformations, for example *Timon of Athens*, refurbished by, among others, Thomas Shadwell in 1678, James Love in 1768, and Richard Cumberland in 1771. Each gave a little more to the new love plot and to the additional female characters; the Cumberland version goes the furthest of these in pathetic displays, ending in the common sentimental tableau of dying father supported by dutiful daughter.

It is undoubtedly the sentimentalization of many traditional plays, as much as the existence of new and pure sentimental drama, that has made the theatrical period from about 1740 to 1780 seem entirely sentimental. Probably it is also due to the propaganda of the most lasting dramatists, Goldsmith and Sheridan, who wished to stress the daring and originality of their oppositional pieces, *She Stoops to Conquer* (1773) and *The School for Scandal* (1777). Yet of the new plays performed during these years R. W. Bevis in *The Laughing Tradition* (1980) has suggested that only about half could be termed sentimental works (although even with this estimate there is a problem since judgement is mainly based on published plays, and playwrights habitually sentimentalized stage works for a reading public attuned to the sentimental novel). As Allardyce Nicoll early noted in his *History of English Drama* (1927), 'when we look at the typical dramatic fare of the period, we may be inclined to wonder whether, after all, it was not sentimentalism which was the fashion insecurely planted in the theatre'.[4]

Although in its purity sentimental drama may have been a minority form, sentimentalism nevertheless clearly touched almost all playwrights, including those who, like Goldsmith and Sheridan, declared themselves against its excesses. On the whole the contemporary perception seems just: that the stage had grown sober and moral, that comedy and tragedy were no longer distinct forms, and that the spectator was asked to attend the theatre to cry and be improved.

Tragedy

With the Restoration theatre, women for the first time came on to the stage. Initially their physical presence was most exploited in bawdy comedy, but, as plays and audiences grew more decorous, theatrical women came to assume something of the moral and pathetic value they were beginning to hold in the culture as a whole. In many plays women became touchstones of morality and fetishized centres of the plot.

The tragedies of the Restoration dramatists, Thomas Southerne, John Banks and Thomas Otway, emphasized the pathos of the situations they presented. Frequently their plays simply aroused pity instead of the mingled pity and terror of traditional tragedy. Otway's *The Orphan* (1680) can exemplify, for Otway became in the eighteenth century the pathetic tragedian *par excellence*; when the poet Collins wrote his 'Ode to Pity' (1746) concerning tragic pathos and pain, Otway was the first modern writer he treated.

The Orphan is a typical Otway production. It tries to give heroic significance to an essentially private tale of familial nastiness and disaster. The plot presents two brothers vying for Monimia, a young girl who has grown up within their family. She enters a secret marriage with one brother but the other, ignorant of the fact, tricks her into lying with him on her wedding night. The act is error not vice and is due to fraternal secrecy not to utter villainy. It is made horrible only by the marriage which turns the fairly insignificant deflowering of a maid into the dishonourable defiling of a wife. In the latter case only the death of the woman can expiate – although seventy years later, in Richardson's more sentimental times, a character in *Sir Charles Grandison* 'thought both brothers deserved to be hanged' as well.

As a pathetic tragedy, *The Orphan* is a hybrid play, mingling the Restoration obsession with sex and gender conflicts with a display of sentimental qualities. The pathetic Monimia, a 'poor and helpless Orphan' is sentimentally gentle, susceptible and soft, but her softness is most manifest in her obtrusive 'white and swelling breasts'. Although she is passive and idealized, she yet utters some of the female complaint at the patriarchal order associated with spirited Restoration heroines, and her male antagonists are equally quick – in a quite unsentimental way – to rail against women. According to Monimia, men aim to 'undo poor/Maids and make our ruin easie', while men state proudly that they are 'false,/ Dissembling, subtle, cruel, and unconstant', and they firmly resist the feminization so much a part of later sentimental drama.

The heroine's fate is, however, unambiguously sentimental. Her body speaks authentically in tears and trembling when she cannot utter a word, and she imagines chastening it into purity after her inadvertent fall, through the proper female method of suffering and madness. By so doing she acquires for herself the high status of victim.

The mingled characteristics of *The Orphan* recur in the she-tragedies of Nicholas Rowe, who sentimentalized tragedy still further in his concentration on the victimized woman. *The Fair Penitent* (1703) pits family sentiment against female sexuality in the manner of Otway and again enacts the replacement of the sexual by the subordinate woman. To a lesser degree it also shows the substitution for the gay Restoration seducer of the filial feminized suitor – the heroine's clear distaste for the latter in this play frees him from any taint of sexuality.

In *The Fair Penitent* the heroine Calista has only two roles open to her before wifehood: virgin or whore. She chooses to be a whore and refuses to become the sign of male honour, insisting that she herself has her own version and will guard it. But, as the play illustrates, Calista's honour is defined only in masculine terms, and the whore's role is powerless in the male scheme since it cannot influence powerful men. Once Calista has given her virginity, she can only weep and rail against 'man, who makes his mirth of our undoing!/ The base professed betrayer of our sex!' In later sentimental works such as *The London Merchant*, the female protest against subordination and reification is commonly given to villains, and the audience is left to decide whether feminist beliefs in purely female standards cause vice or the reverse. In this early play, the heroine herself still rages against male dominance. Yet, despite her protests, Calista, like Monimia before her, must in the end accept. In her imagination she chastens her wickedly sexual body so that it may regain its sentimental meaning; in reality she follows Monimia into the appropriate suicide, so reconstructing herself as distressed lady and victim.

The prologue to *The Fair Penitent* claimed that the play was a tale of private woes 'like your own'; the struggle of domesticity against sexuality was indeed common and yet the characters were said to be noble and distant, as in traditional tragedy. So too in *The Orphan* the setting was high although the characters were bound in a private family, the cause of the play's success according to Samuel Richardson. Lillo's *The London Merchant* (1731) is a rare attempt in English to make a clear connection between sentiment and the bourgeoisie (although this became usual in later German drama) and to make a central issue of the ethical values – duty and probity – of the trading middle class.

Lillo saw himself as an heir of Otway and Rowe. Like theirs, his play aims at a single emotional response in the audience but goes beyond them in explicitly claiming a moral, didactic purpose: it wants to fill the eyes with tears for, according to the sentimental theory, weeping eyes show and encourage 'a gen'rous sense of others' woe'. To this end it eschews dramatic realism and lets its hero Barnwell, as soon as he is accused of murder, directly address the audience: 'Be warned, ye youths, who see my sad despair.'

This use of dramatic speech, less for characterization and plot than for its ethical content, with the audience rather than another character as recipient, is common in sentimental plays, which therefore require a double response in the spectator: at times they must be taken as vehicles of dramatic utterances and at other times as purveyors of moral propositions. Failure to distinguish between the two required responses can result in pointless criticism, for example that a particular sentimental character is unpleasantly priggish and self-deceiving.[5]

The London Merchant is a more thoroughgoing sentimental work than the plays of Otway and Rowe, and it breaks more clearly with heroic tragedy by employing prose. It uses to the full the sentimental techniques of pathetic tableaux, painful reversals and stock good and bad characters. Like *The Fair Penitent* it pits the familial feminine virtues of compassion and submission against extra-familial passion and sexuality. The hero should be a fraternal lover to a passive, daughterly female, but instead he associates with an active Restoration kind of woman, who flatly refuses the proper feminine image of the sentimental lady: 'that imaginary being is an emblem of thy cursed sex collected. A mirror wherein each particular man may see his own likeness and that of all mankind.' Worse, against the Shaftesburian order of benevolence and harmony, she urges a view closer to Hobbes and Mandeville: 'All actions seem alike natural and indifferent to man and beast, who devour, or are devoured, as they meet with others weaker or stronger than themselves.'

The play details Barnwell's fall from commercial and domestic grace through the evil woman's agency, and his just and pathetic punishment. The values to which Barnwell succumbs are allowed a hearing in the play but in the end they are entirely obliterated by sentimental morality. The work refuses to be dialectical, retreating from a complexity it occasionally comes close to allowing in its presentation of the hero's perverse inability to act from gratitude and in its depiction of the difficulties of the knowing woman. The death of Barnwell is justified and aestheticized, and the tearful, pathetic response he insists on evoking in the spectators makes them echo the forgiveness he achieves within the play and so avoid horror at his quite enormous crimes. This forgiveness is consonant with Barnwell's avoidance of any tragic grandeur through the construction of his character and through his indulgence in an exemplary self-abasement. Together with the understanding of his basic goodness of heart in spite of these crimes, this forgiveness by the spectators in no way prevents their accepting the justice of the law that refuses to excuse Barnwell on sentimental grounds and so condemns him to death.

The pathetic domestic tragedy of Lillo has only a few successors in England in the mid-century, one being Edward Moore's *The Gamester* (1753), which at the end addresses the audience thus: 'Let frailer Minds take Warning; and from Example learn, that Want of Prudence is Want of Virtue.' The play has the sentimental plot of *The London Merchant*, wherein a weak man is led astray and ends condemned by the law. In this case, however, the hero is wrongly accused of the crime, and the pathos of his suicide in prison is exaggerated by news of his release and of a legacy he has thrown away that would have saved him from poverty. Marmontel's description at the beginning of the introduction suggests the pathetic power, for an eighteenth-century audience, of this sort of plot.

In both *The London Merchant* and *The Gamester* the main characters are men, although they are flanked by distressed, virtuous ladies. In their subordination to more powerful figures and in their inability to help themselves or direct their fate, these men assume something of the female role of victim. Yet they cannot entirely follow the main female trajectory, which passes through degradation and self-abasement through the sexual fall before the final pathos of an undeserved but necessary death. Consequently there is a tendency for plays about pathetic heroes to become sensational and extreme in their plots. This tendency can be well appreciated in *The Mysterious Husband* (1783) by Richard Cumberland, probably the main professor of sentimental tragedy in the last part of the century and consciously the heir of Lillo and Moore.

The complicated plot of *The Mysterious Husband* revolves around Lord Davenant, a widower who has remarried a virtuous woman. Although she has always loved another, she is entirely faithful to her new husband. He, however, has formerly wedded Marianne, a young woman for whom he still yearns but who, assuming him dead because of his long absence, herself remarries. Marianne is the sister of Lady Davenant's beloved and her new husband is Lord Davenant's son. When this family complexity is revealed, the son is horrified to discover he has married his father's wife and, in the confusion of guilt that follows, Lord Davenant kills himself. The incestuous sensationalism here largely prevents any tragic response in the audience, and the repentance of the villain before he kills himself makes his violent death a strange mingling of sinful but heroic action and pathetic sentimental suicide.

In 1794 Cumberland produced *The Jew*, a comedy which demanded a change of heart in the audience towards a victimized group. From Steele onwards sentimental drama had concerned itself with social problems such as gambling and duelling, but in the 1790s it also appropriated humanitarian issues such as slavery, the treatment of war victims and the incarceration of debtors. Such issues were especially the province of women playwrights such as Marianna Starke and Maria Barrell. In *The Captive* (1790) the latter aimed to expose the sorry condition of debtors imprisoned for many years for debts which they had no chance of paying. The play works entirely through conventional sentimental tableaux, the supreme one echoing *The Gamester* in presenting a husband dying in prison surrounded by a virtuous wife and faithful servant.

Maria Barrell wrote her play while herself in the King's Bench. She was composing, she declared, surrounded by the 'gloomy walls of a prison' with a 'mind wounded by disappointment, and harrassed by scenes of sorrow almost incredible'. A prologue enforces the distressing image: she is 'a captive stranger in her native land,/ While by her widow'd side two Orphans wait'. Here Maria Barrell insists on making her own sorry situation part of her written play text, a less common habit among dramatists than among novelists and poets, who often presented themselves as distressed parents or sensitive recluses in rural retreats.

Comedy

As in tragedy, sentimental qualities crept gradually into comedy, which became a popular sentimental form since dramatists seemed to enjoy rewarding virtue materially, as Richardson did in *Pamela*. The qualities early appeared in the works of the canny dramatist Colley Cibber, who extolled plays depicting 'Truth and Human Life' and provoking tears in the audience. Although many of the humorous and titillating elements of Restoration comedy continued in this drama, he stated that his primary aim was to reform the spectators through example, and he provided many sententious tags for them to take away and memorize. In the dedication of *The Careless Husband* (1704) and in his *Apology* (1740), he stressed that he had always had 'the interest and honour of virtue in view'. To which end virtue in misfortune had been preferred in his plays to greatness in distress. For readers who wish to judge and mock predominantly sentimental characters with naturalistic and psychological criteria, Cibber provides wonderful examples. A famous one is a scene in *The Careless Husband* (1704) in which a virtuous wife, finding her husband asleep in an adulterous and chilly situation, converts him to virtue with an act of selflessness, whereby she places her own garment on his bared head; thus she protects him from the cold and at the same time lets him know she knows.

Pope made Colley Cibber the main target of *The Dunciad* but he spared some abuse for other semi-sentimental playwrights such as Susanna Centlivre. Like Cibber, Centlivre was transitional, vacillating between laughing satiric and sentimental codes. In 1700 in the preface to her first play, *The Perjur'd Husband*, for example, she chafed against Collier's demands for chaste language in the theatre, noting the absurdity of making a lewd woman speak 'in the Words of a Psalm'; in the same year she wrote in a letter that the 'main design of Comedy, is to make us laugh'.[6] Three years later in the preface to *Love's Contrivance*, Centlivre followed opinion and affirmed that she 'took peculiar Care to dress my Thoughts in such a modest Stile that it might not give Offence to any'. In *The Gamester* (1705), a partial relapse into the laughing mode, she yet hopes 'to divert without that Vicious Strain, which usually attends the Comick Muse' and she aims to 'recommend Morality'. As in many sentimental comedies, Centlivre's characters suddenly reform through example, and the audience learns appropriate response to the final pathetic show of repentance.

Pope no doubt despised Susanna Centlivre for her sentimental attitudes and Whig politics. But he had an added reason for contempt in her sex. He linked her with other women writers of the Restoration and Queen Anne years, Aphra Behn, Delarivière Manley and Eliza Haywood, who seemed to be improperly penetrating male culture. Such penetration signalled for Pope a breakdown of traditional standards, while sentimentalism itself, implicated in this breakdown, was regarded as an unfortunate feminization of culture. The association of women's values and women's writing with sentimentalism would be a cause of anxiety for male dramatists throughout the sentimental period, and there is much protestation that tears and compassion are actually signs of true manliness.

Steele favourably reviewed both Centlivre and Cibber. In his notice of *The Careless Husband* in the *Tatler* (1704) he praised the sentimental elements, especially the elevation of domestic affections and virtuous innocence:

> It has in it all the reverent offices of life, such as regard to parents, husbands, and honourable lovers, preserved with the utmost care, and at the same time that agreeableness of behaviour, with the intermixture of pleasing passions, which arise from innocence and virtue interspersed in such a manner as that to be charming and agreeable shall appear the natural consequence of being virtuous.

The great promoter and popularizer of sentimental moral comedy and the Shaftesburian notion of virtue, Steele exhibits his own predilections and habits as a playwright in his praise of Cibber. Although finding Jeremy Collier overharsh in his criticism of the contemporary stage, Steele likewise attacked its bawdry and immorality and in *The Lying Lover* (1703) he claimed that he intended 'to write a *Comedy* in the Severity [Collier] required'. *Tatler* articles blamed Wycherley for abetting adultery in his plays and Etherege for writing a work with 'nothing in it but what is built upon the ruin of virtue and innocence'. Instead, Steele asked for explicitly didactic plays which would encourage virtue and 'strip Vice of the gay Habit in which it has too long appear'd'. What Steele espoused has something formally in common with tragicomedy as theorized by the Italian Giambattista Guarini in 1601: a theatre that deals with private actions, and demands the emotional participation of the audience, while eschewing the subjection to tragic catharsis. Such theatre also pulls away from the laughing response: comedy, Steele considered, need not always be comic – indeed he preferred a comedy of 'joy too exquisite for laughter'.

Steele's last play, *The Conscious Lovers*, contains both quick and lively dialogue and the didactic thrust he demanded of comedy. It provides the audience with exemplary types: Young Bevil, 'an obedient and grateful son', Indiana, a 'wretched, helpless . . . orphan', Sealand, an honest kindly merchant, and Humphrey, a faithful old retainer, 'more like an humble friend than a servant'. The plot is the long-lost child one, ending in the tableau of father–daughter reunion. The lovers' complications are unthreatening, since almost all involved have good hearts, the seemingly harsh father working only to test his son and the suspicious aunt acting primarily for the protection of her niece.

Sentiments in the play are delivered mainly through Young Bevil, many of whose utterances, like those of *The London Merchant*, are clearly not intended to contribute to his character but to present aphorisms directly to the audience – 'to convince is much more than to conquer' – or press on them social advice about how to treat servants and inferiors and to avoid duelling with honour. Young Bevil also teaches the spectators the sentimental doctrine of pleasure through virtue: 'how great a pleasure is it to him who has a true taste of life to ease an aching heart, to see the human countenance lighted up into smiles of joy.' Expressing the common anxiety that such benevolent virtue may seem effeminate, Steele firmly announces that nothing in fact could be more manly.

Within *The Conscious Lovers* an opera is approved called 'Griselda', which concerns 'the distress of an injured, innocent woman'. This is the archetypal situation for the lady of sensibility and it is not an especially comic one. So the play has some difficulty containing within its comic bounds the sighing orphan Indiana, who responds to bodily rather than verbal expressiveness and who insists on living entirely contingently: 'All the rest of my life is but waiting till he comes. I only live when I'm with him.' Towards the close of the play when she thinks she may be balked of her love, just before the sentimental reversal that will bring everyone into tearful familial community, Indiana suddenly breaks the light-hearted tone of the play to display herself as a sentimental victim adrift in a she-tragedy, and she prepares to embrace the immoderate fate envisaged by Monimia and Calista, to 'sigh and weep, to rave, run wild, a lunatic in chains or hid in darkness, [to] mutter in distracted starts and broken accents'. And she moans that all her comfort 'must be to expostulate in madness, to relieve with frenzy my despair, and shrieking to demand of fate why – why was

I born to such variety of sorrows!' The stress on providential activity that closes the play cannot entirely obliterate this clichéd but contextually striking outburst, which gives to *The Conscious Lovers* as a whole something of the uneasiness of a mingled rather than mixed genre and points to the instability of sentimentalism itself when embodied in the comic plot.

Clearly Steele was aware of the sentimental fractures in the comic surface of his plays, for he wrote of such a fracturing in his *Lying Lover*, in which a man belatedly reforms:

> The anguish he there expresses, and the mutual sorrow between an only child and a tender father in that distress are, perhaps, an injury to the rules of comedy but I am sure they are a justice to those of morality.

The morality which is seemingly injurious to comedy is delivered through the didactic and undramatic sentiments, such as those of Young Bevil, scattered throughout Steele's plays, to such an extent that Hazlitt termed them 'homilies in dialogue'; it also comes through the pathos of the distressed Indiana and of the father in *The Lying Lover*, which jerks virtuous tears from the audience. The theory here, a complicated one, suggests that this tearful response to pathos gives to the spectator a sense of self-worth, of self-approval: 'generous pity of a painted woe/ Makes us ourselves both more approve and know' (epilogue of *The Lying Lover*). This self-approval based on pity is declared to be ultimately outward-looking and unselfish, finding expression in acts of benevolence. Laughing comedy in contrast, Steele argues, gives an audience a sense of 'sudden self-esteem' which in time leads to self-contempt.

Obviously such an ethical-psychological dramatic theory could be attacked as complacent self-justification or even hypocrisy, but John Gay in *The Present State of Wit* (1711) pays tribute to what he apprehends as the actual moral effect of Steele's plays on his contemporaries outside the theatre:

> It would have been a jest, some time since, for a Man to have asserted that any thing Witty could be said in praise of a Marry'd State, or that Devotion and Virtue were any way necessary to the Character of a fine Gentleman . . . . Instead of complying with the false Sentiments or Vicious tasts of the Age . . . [Steele] has boldly assur'd them, that they were altogether in the wrong, and commanded them, with an Authority, which perfectly well

became him, to surrender themselves to his Arguments for Virtue and Good Sense. (pp. 3–4)

Yet, despite the decided moral emphasis in Steele's plays, the speedy development of sentimental expression soon made even these works appear insufficiently sentimental. If *The Tender Husband* (1705) ends in the spectacle of a weeping and submissive lady, it none the less begins with a transvestite scene and a promise of adultery. Richardson's Pamela did not at all approve of the piece and thought ill of the summary nature of the repentance it delivers; in *Clarissa* a copy of Steele's plays has found its way into the library of the villainous bawd Mrs Sinclair.

By the mid- to late eighteenth century comedy was felt to have abandoned the satiric for the sentimental mode. Yet on a cline from sentiment to satire, most plays would rest somewhere in the middle, with many seemingly oppositional ones like *She Stoops to Conquer* and *The School for Scandal* enclosing sentimental elements, and many primarily sentimental pieces including some satire. As in tragedy, so in comedy, Cumberland can exemplify the predominantly sentimental mode, with comedies moving towards, if never achieving, sentimental purity.

Cumberland's comedies such as *The Carmelite* (1784) or *The West Indian* (1771) are aimed at the heart. They display their morality at the expense of characterization and of any attempt at realism of plot. They present emotional over narrative complexity, and turn less on events or psychological disturbances than on tableaux of familial sorrow and joy, of the recognition of mother, father and son, and of the happy realization of the filial bond. In the plays of Cumberland and others, the hero and heroine are frequently innocents from the country or from foreign primitive parts where they have escaped the corruption of metropolitan society. They experience a somehow ennobling poverty as a test of worth and they escape it not through activity but through a sudden providential inheritance. Often the reversal is brought about by the good merchant, a figure much idealized in sentimental drama, as suggested by *The London Merchant* and *The Conscious Lovers*, and friendship is again highly extolled. Morality is clearly expressed as generosity and benevolence in men, and as virginity and compassion in women, and a feeling heart and delicate sensibility are prized in both. Villainy hardly exists since, if the heart is right, a person can reform simply by being moved at an affecting sight, and faults can be forgiven on the show of a tear. Although the early sentimental opposition of familial and sexual is less evident and more delicately suggested in Cumberland, his plays continue to enact the old plot of sentiment, the defeat in life or death of the wickedly cynical by the simply virtuous; meanwhile a frequent denouement is the renewed assertion of the filial tie and the assurance that the hero, despite irregularities, has 'a heart beaming with benevolence'.

Although a woman playwright was no oddity by the close of the eighteenth century, the sentimental matter and its association with femininity ensured that an appealing issue could be made of the writer's gender. So George Colman's epilogues to Elizabeth Inchbald's plays insist that the author is a woman and use the fact decorously to claim equal literary treatment and opportunity for female writers. Indeed, if feeling is the basis of art, as many critics from Dennis onwards held, then women whose '*Heart* . . . with Passions is stor'd' should be the best fitted for writing and their works should have sincerity, the true tone of sensibility. Colman, however, catches the ambiguous status of the female writer in the context of the sentimental construction of woman – endowed with superior sensibility but advised to be utterly subordinate – when he both asserts the woman's pre-eminence in feeling and pathos, and yet terms the female author a 'weak Woman'.

Inchbald's *I'll Tell You What* (1786) mingles elements in a way very similar to Steele's *Conscious Lovers* at the beginning of the century. Although it has lively women, one erring and finally repentant and the other virtuous and spirited, it also displays a true sentimental lady in distress, whose misery, like Indiana's, thoroughly disturbs the comic mode. This lady eschews the pertness of her sisters and instead reveals 'sensibility in her countenance . . . blushes on her cheek – tears in her eyes . . . a tremor in her voice'. She is animated by pathetic tenderness and prepared to sacrifice her virtue to maternal devotion, a sacrifice that would in this late sentimental work be deemed forgivable since it was inspired by sensibility, 'the sudden starts . . . formed by the excessive anguish of the soul'. Because of the deflection from traditional intrigue comedy, the denouement is less concerned with sorting out comic mistakes and differences than with the familial tableaux that marked sentimental drama from the start – of father and son and of husband and wife, caught in an ecstasy of weeping and kneeling; lest the scenes seem too feminine, there is, as in

Steele's and countless other plays, stress on the manliness of masculine tears flowing, unlike women's, 'from so deep a source'.

The sentimental elements in Inchbald's plays and in her image as a female writer are obtrusive, and yet in these later offerings there are modifying tendencies. *I'll Tell You What*, for example, praises sentimental domesticity and the distressed lady, but allows another virtuous heroine to be superior in sense and common sense as well as sensibility; she approaches less the female victim than the new heroine emerging in the anti-sentimental novels of Jane Austen and Maria Edgeworth.

And the author herself is not always presented with 'Heart'. In Maria Barrell's *The Captive*, the image of the playwright which was delivered in the prologue was suitably constructed for the pathetic material to follow in the drama, but often eighteenth-century prologues worked against not with the pathos of a play by, for instance, giving a knowingness and implied cynicism to the actress playing the pathetic part and speaking the epilogue. In Inchbald's *Every One Has His Fault* (1793), the sentimental mask is snatched off the woman author by the male prologue writer who begs that she may not be 'Confin'd entirely to domestic arts,/Producing only children, pies and tarts'. With its exaltation of domesticity and sacred motherhood, the true sentimental spirit would be aghast at such a mocking miscellany of bakery and offspring.

IV *Poetry*

By the 1740s a poetry associated with moralizing, with natural description and close delineation of mental states, especially the melancholic and the anxiously pious, had grown extremely popular in England. Since the period was an expansive and active one in economic and political terms, this sort of inward-looking, self-conscious verse became an especially suitable medium for marginal women, who wrote it in increasing numbers, and for men who, in their hypochondria, melancholia, sleeplessness or laziness, were in some way at odds with the energy if not the values of their society.

Devotional and meditative verse

Sentimental habits and techniques entered religious verse of all kinds, especially the new genre of the vernacular congregational hymn developed through Dissent and Methodism. The hymns of the Methodist revival are less confessions or songs of praise than efforts properly to align the emotions of the singers and teach the feeling heart, presumed in everyone, a correct response – rather in the manner of contemporary sentimental drama. Many of Charles Wesley's 9000 hymns are evangelical tools aimed at conversion, written not for regular church services but for the emotional happenings of field meetings. His hymns tell of sudden, extreme transitions from despair to ecstasy and they express emotions in the broken speech patterns typical of sentimental literature. Feeling is exalted in these hymns as both provoking and responding to salvation; it is a means of grace and a method of direct communication with God who is a felt presence in the human sigh and in the 'inner groaning and crying':

> Thy tender Heart is still the same,
>   And melts at Human Woe:
> JESU, for Thee distrest I am,
>   I want Thy love to know.[1]

In such verse God becomes a friendly Shaftesburian, while Jesus acquires the kindly qualities of the Man of Feeling.[2]

Protestant devotion was also displayed in a rhapsodical kind of poetry, in tone resembling the work of Madame Guyon, who exulted in her sensational humility before God, and of Jacob Boehme, who ecstatically proclaimed the world's harmony with the divine mind. Much religious verse conflated the trembling feelings of sensibility with the orthodox experience of divine love and conveyed this conflation in an erotically charged, repetitive style. In the early part of the century Elizabeth Rowe desired to express her religious experience 'with all the melting language lovers use/ To tell their pain, or speak their rising joy', her piety is delivered to the reader in terms of panting breasts, languishings and tender feelings.

Religious meditative rather than devotional verse is less concerned with love than with death. In Robert Blair's 'The Grave' (1743) this is still primarily physical in the first half of the poem – 'the gloomy horrors of the tomb' and 'vaults/ Furred round with mouldy damps and ropy slime'. But in other writers it appears less a physical than an emotional and sensational experience, a kind of Gothic fear or fascination. Death-obsessed poems describe in detail both the mood of anxiety over the coming annihilation and the escapist longing for the absolute passivity and extreme susceptibility expressed in death. The complete contrasts typical of sentimental verse are illustrated in this meditative poetry through the sudden intrusions of death into life, while the sentimental tableaux depict virtuous and vicious dying.[3]

The poet, usually male, contemplates death in a darkening

world, having retreated from public life into a region that provides no social and almost no physical context for the self. He is aware both of his trembling and susceptible heart and of the dwindling light on the landscape. The poetry so produced is part of the elegiac tradition of English literature, taking something in mood and convention from the poetry of rural retreat stretching back to Virgil and Horace and something from Milton's 'Il Penseroso', so loved by sentimentalists in the eighteenth century. It differs from earlier verse, however, in the assumption that its melancholy suggests a superior and valuable sensibility, which, although it leads initially to withdrawal and solitude, should result in benevolence to mankind.

In the eighteenth century, the disorder of melancholy was explained and described through a variety of biological constructions, in all of which, from black bile to acid vapours, there is emphasis on darkness. As Michel Foucault wrote in *Madness and Civilization*, in eighteenth-century melancholy the spirits were thought to be

> charged with darkness; they become 'obscure, opaque, shadowy'; and the images of things which they bear to the brain and to the mind are veiled with 'shadows and with shades.' They become heavy and closer to a dark chemical vapour than to pure light. (p. 120)

The poets Collins and Cowper were labelled as melancholically mad, but, even in poets never termed insane, the occasional withdrawal into a solipsistic state, where the external world is obliterated in darkness or opacity, whatever the final social result allies them to sufferers of melancholia. Such an alliance helped to give the disease in its less extreme forms a kind of literary prestige among the educated. But it lacked attraction for Pope, and his image of the final overpowering darkness at the end of *The Dunciad* is his comment on the private, enthusiastic and melancholic temperament; Edward Young, whose *Night Thoughts* (1742–6) aims to outwing 'the midnight raven' and take its 'gloomy flight' beyond the light of the world, might have been his model.

Young's long poem is tense, like much writing influenced by sentimental thought. It expresses the emotional religious fervor of Methodism, while emphasizing the sentimental qualities of benevolence and pity, and it exalts social sympathy and fellowship in the manner of Shaftesbury and Hume, while yearning for isolation from human contact. Praise is given to society and domestic affections, but the poet himself is alone, withdrawn, sleepless and unconversing.

Another sort of tension comes from Young's Newtonian enthusiasm for the world, which had difficulty comprehending the negative orthodoxies of Christianity. The poet trumpeted his joy in the sensation of the universe, especially the vastness Newton revealed – the 'mathematic glories of the skies' – a joy similar to Addison's when he described the great in nature: at the same time he felt a Christian apprehension of earth as transient and negative. God was both excitingly vast and vastly distant from humanity.

In response to his speculations, his sense of hugeness and his consciousness of his own isolated, worrying, unsleeping and melancholic self, Young shows the affective symptoms of the sentimentalist; he trembles, flinches and exclaims: 'Thought wanders up and down, surprised, aghast,/And wond'ring at her own: how reason reels!' Often he moves into the rhapsodic mode of Shaftesbury, often he is simply breathless.

Yet *Night Thoughts* is ultimately not inward- but outward-looking. The aim is not individual self-analysis but emotional instruction and Young's methods are those common to writers of other forms of sentimental literature, personification, tableaux and images of contrast: 'How groaning hospitals eject their dead!/What numbers, once in Fortune's lap high-fed,/Solicit the cold hand of Charity!'

Poetry of poetic sensibility

When the religious validation or belief is less clear than it is in Young, the meditative poetry reveals more explicitly the self-consciousness always involved. Thomas Gray records the bitterness that creeps into melancholic graveyard poetry when the sense of heaven is less pressing and when the retreat from humanity seems not so much a removal to contemplate mortality and the joys of heaven as a fear of the darkness of death.

In Gray's poetry, sensibility exaggerates and sensationalizes inevitable earthly disappointment and decay. In 'Ode on a Distant Prospect of Eton College' (1747), the poet with his 'weary soul' sees the happy children dramatically as victims surrounded by 'black Misfortune's baleful train' of jealousy, fear, despair, scorn, remorse, madness and poverty. All are condemned to misery, 'The tender for another's pain/ Th'unfeeling for his own'.

At the end of the second version of 'Elegy Written in a Country Churchyard' (1751), Gray focuses on the predicament of a poetic youth all forlorn and 'woeful wan', whom Melancholy marked for its own and who 'gained from heav'n ('twas all he wished) a friend'. Here sensibility is clearly tied to the melancholic poet, the unhappy solitary genius who is an innocent in a vicious world, described in archaic Renaissance vocabulary that associates him with the past rather than with the bustling present. Poets who seemed to eighteenth-century readers to fit this image formed a tradition and became predictable types of vulnerable sensibility: Milton, Otway, Collins and Chatterton. Such poets were supremely men of feeling, feeling more intense than that possessed by ordinary men and inevitably isolating since it was the emotional stance not its skilful verbal expression that was stressed. For William Cowper the poetic process itself seemed both to isolate and to mitigate isolation; 'poetic pains' separated the poet from the world and made him acutely aware of evanescence, of 'the fleeting images that fill/The mirror of the mind'.

In 1770 Thomas Chatterton killed himself at the age of 17. In the late eighteenth century, poetic sensibility seemed especially validated by suicide. Thomas Warton's 'The Suicide' (1777) proclaims that the dead man was urged to his deed not by ineffectuality or irreligious despair but by 'many a feeling too refin'd' and a too 'wakeful sense of woe'. The supreme exponent of sensibility as suicide was of course Werther, the prose creation of Goethe, but the association with poetry was ensured by a host of poetic imitators such as Amelia Pickering and Charlotte Smith who vibrated to the hero's fate and versified his melancholia.

In mid-eighteenth-century poetry, the poet's creative function was sentimentalized into extra sensitive response. If creativity was an expression of the emotion of joy, similar according to Shaftesbury to the joy of a creative God in the uncreated forms of things, then the poet's feeling becomes all-important. A procession of lone enthusiasts, like James Beattie's 'Minstrel' (1771), listen to 'the roar/ Of the wide-weltering waves' and reveal their special and refined sensibility, while Collins in his 'Ode to Fear' (1746) displays his 'throbbing heart' as proof of poetic fear and glories in his surrender to 'ecstatic Wonder'.

Sensitivity is the supreme quality in the poet, whether to 'Pale

Grief', or 'pleasing Pain', the pain being as essential as the pleasure since it renders bliss more exquisite and response more sensitive. Misery or adversity can, it was thought, be converted into pleasure by the sensitive poetical mind in two ways. First it educates sympathy: in Gray's 'Ode to Adversity' (1753) it makes the sufferer 'melt at others' woe', rather as the dramatic representation had done, and this sentimental melting is clearly felt as pleasurable. Second it educates the aesthetic sense by making the sufferer more aware of joy and pain and so more understanding of the aesthetic whole of human life, similar to the aesthetic whole of nature, which can harmonize horrific chasms and smiling plains. So adversity, like Joy, can deliver tears that are 'sadly-pleasing'. The idea is captured in Gray's 'Ode on the Pleasure Arising from Vicissitude' (1775) where the poet argues that the human mind, able to remember and project from past experience, can uniquely aestheticize present experience:

> The hues of bliss more brightly glow,
> Chastis'd by subtler tints of woe:
> And blended form, with artful strife,
> The strength and harmony of life.

Because sensitivity was so prized as the source of the poetic faculty, spontaneity in creation became a necessary quality of poetry. The figure of the Aeolian harp which sings God-given music spontaneously was deployed for the artist's function and it became commonplace as a metaphor for the responsive sentimental poet in the work of Thomson, Akenside, Gray, Collins and Macpherson. In Joseph Warton's 'Ode to Fancy' the 'enthusiastic maid' of poetry rather than the skilled and conscious poet plays on the 'sacred string' of the harp.

The purpose of such spontaneous art is, naturally enough, spontaneous reading: readers are taught by the poet's stance within the poem how to surrender to the work. In 'Ode to Fancy' they are further instructed in affective and enraptured response through the poet's plea to poetry to reign over, to overwhelm, to shake and to move the passions: 'O'er all our list'ning passions reign,/ O'erwhelm our souls with joy and pain,/With terror shake and pity move.' In Thomas Warton's 'The Pleasures of Melancholy' (1747), the reader, with the poet, must display a 'breast/ That pants with wild astonishment and love'.

Nature poetry

The inspiration and cause of much of the exemplary rapture and palpitation in the sensitive poet and his sensitive reader is the nature revealed anew by Newton's scientific discoveries. To the earlier eighteenth-century authors, unlike the Romantic poets, this observed and intuited world appeared wonderfully mechanistic and awe-inspiring in its government by natural laws and in its diversity yet 'silent harmony'. Since human beings were helped to pleasurable response to the natural mechanical world by being endowed with God's faculty to transform it to their own satisfaction, it was right and devotional to study and praise the 'varied God' through varied nature. Nowhere is this more resoundingly and influentially expressed than in James Thomson's *The Seasons*, the writing and changing of which spanned two decades from the 1720s to the 1740s.

Thomson, whom Collins named 'Nature's child', was much impressed by Newton's optics and physics, 'the blaze/Of truth'. He praised the 'unprofuse magnificence divine' which called 'from a few causes such a scheme of things . . . an universe complete!' Because of this connection with divinity, he accepted that the natural world, like the human body in later sentimental writing, had a kind of authenticity. Material nature therefore did not need conscious mental human mediation and should be considered and described for itself; Thomson sought to convey in his poetry not memory or previous renderings of nature but its present experience.

But Thomson also accepted that the human mind constructed its own aesthetic apprehension of this world and he was much concerned with natural phenomena as promoters of subjective experience. So he lingered on mountains and mists, for example, which inspired in humanity feelings of harmony, melancholy and 'pleasing dread'. Like Addison, who had associated English fog and mist with the melancholia and fantastical imaginings of English poets, Thomson was fascinated by obscure atmospherics, with vapours, clouds and storms, which 'exalt the soul to solemn thought'. In 'Winter' the declining year gives 'philosophic melancholy' to 'the secret soul'.

Like the later moral philosophers, whose Scottish, non-metropolitan and middle-class background he shared, Thomson admired Shaftesbury, whom he called 'the friend of man' and whom he described as charming the heart of his reader with 'moral beauty'. Especially impressed by Shaftesbury's ideas of sympathy and aesthetic morality, Thomson saw nature leading to virtue and social harmony. As he wrote in the Preface to the second edition of 'Winter' (1726), 'I know no subject more elevating . . . more ready to awake the poetical enthusiasm, the philosophical reflection, and the moral sentiment, than the works of Nature'; he found in them 'all that enlarges and transports the soul'.

Above all, Thomson saw nature as a vehicle for the human spirit to travel to God, a rather unspecific but well-meaning deity mocked by the Anglo-Catholic critic, Hoxie Neale Fairchild, as a kind of Cheshire Cat, of whom all has faded 'except the cosmic grin'.[4] Nature caused 'heavenly musing' and bore 'the swelling thought aloft to heaven'. Especially efficacious were 'the grand works of Nature' which, according to his letter to David Mallet, raised and animated 'by moral and sublime reflections'. Vast phenomena spoke of the vastness of God to finite beings.[5]

Like Young, Thomson is riddled with the contradictions of sentimentalism when it is expressed in imaginative or narrative rather than philosophical form. Sharing the anti-aristocratic bias of so many writers attracted to sentimental attitudes, he is drawn to the lively economic bustle of bourgeois commerce and also to quiescent retreat into unproductive regions, so typical of mid-eighteenth-century poetry. He exults in the world and yet yearns for solitude and retirement which, paradoxically, deliver the social virtues.[6] Nature is appreciated as a vital process in plants, in animals and in human fellowship, and also as a promoter of poetic melancholy and withdrawal. It is in unison with human spectators and contributory to their emotions and yet will not always be internalized by them. And, despite rhapsodies on the beneficent deity expressed in the harmony of natural forms and the providential scheme assumed for humanity, Thomson gives room in his poetry to the experiential, unassimilable pain of the world:

> can human hearts endure
> Th'assembled mischiefs that besiege them round:
> Unlist'ning hunger, fainting weariness,
> The roar of winds and waves, the crush of ice.

In these circumstances a human response cannot be simply exultation in nature and the 'varied God', but 'the tender pang, the pitying tear,/ The sigh for suffering worth'.

The emotional response to nature and nature's God continues through the century in scores of minor poets. Mark Akenside in *The Pleasures of Imagination* (1744), for example, a poetic rendering of many of Addison's points, echoes Thomson in seeing love of nature as a movement towards and a participation in God: 'the men/ Whom nature's works can charm, with God himself/ Hold converse.' Akenside writes much of the effect of the 'complicated joy' derived from grand objects and insists on its egalitarian availability to all men, even to those denied 'Patrician treasures or imperial state'. In 'The Pleasures of Melancholy', Thomas Warton turns on nature 'th'ecstatic eye' and asserts its ability 'to raise, to soothe, to harmonize the mind'. In Gray's 'Ode on the Pleasure arising from Vicissitude', the sense of harmony in nature appreciated by the human mind is conveyed in the image so often employed for the spontaneous poet, the Aeolian instrument: 'nature strikes the lyre,/ And leads the gen'ral song'.

Primitive poetry

Spontaneity was necessary for poetry, the sensitive person was felt to be naturally poetic, and the frequent inspiration of poetry was the natural world. Consequently poetry in its purity should spring from the most primitive and untrained rustics, who would be spontaneously sensitive in apprehension of nature and tenderly sentimental in response to people. Such expectation, fed by the Rousseauist notion of the unspoilt, noble savage, produced a desire for a poetry of sensibility which would be written both by contemporary primitives such as peasants, serving women and slaves, and by ancient primitives, bards from the heroic and barbaric past, free from a classical education and neoclassical restraint. William Duff claimed in his *Essay* of 1767 that original genius would be most vigorous in 'early and uncultivated periods'.

The desire for peasant and menial poetry was partially met by a thick procession of much touted but quickly abandoned poets from the lower orders, who included the servant Mary Leapor, the thresher Stephen Duck, the milkmaid Ann Yearsley and the slave Phyllis Wheatley. Although this line finally produced the major poets, Robert Burns and John Clare, on the whole it was vitiated by the expectations that brought it into being. The work of such marginal men and women tended to be utterly conventional in terms of established writing because such writing presented for its exponents both the excitement of culture and a seeming method of social ascent. At the same time several poets opportunistically gloried in and expanded on their simple image of humble and spontaneous singer: 'unadorned by art, unaccomplished by science', as Ann Yearsley proudly described herself.

Meanwhile, the little spontaneity there was tended to be problematic for the upper and middle classes who patronized the poetry. Often it consisted not of the expected sentimental effusions but of outbursts against the social order and against the poet's sorry predicament as a semi-cultured person trapped in the illiterate peasant class; writing from the workhouse, Ann Candler commented on her fellows: 'Uncultivated, void of sense,/ Unsocial, insincere,/ Their rude behaviour gives offence,/ Their language wounds the ear.'[7] Or the spontaneity might take the form of an intrusion of vulgar dialect and local expression into the conventional styles, an intrusion that was often shown the door by the editors and publishers on whom the rustic poets depended.

The true primitive and spontaneous voice was sought in the past as well as the present, both through the recovery of old forms and through their imitation. The ballad is an example. In the early eighteenth century the modern sentimental as opposed to the folk ballad developed. David Mallet's 'William and Margaret' (1723), for instance, has the common folk theme of love and death but, in its telling of how the slighted woman returns from death to berate her faithless man, the emphasis is less on event in the traditional ballad manner than on the fearful death and on the sensational response of the quaking and raving lover.

By the late decades of the century, ballads were being written above all for pathos, and the ancient form was used to exhibit the pathetic tableaux of domestic grief common to sentimental literature in general. Helen Maria Williams's youthful 'Edwin and Eltruda' is a ballad on the usual subject of fatal love, but its concerns are entirely sentimental; it mocks acreage and wealth, praises the 'gen'rous ample heart', sees courtship as a sighing over fallen birds and a nursing of dead flowers, and climaxes in the tableau of daughter and dying father.

At the same time the folk ballad iself, with its spare narrative and bare diction, was sentimentally refurbished. In the *Spectator* Addison had praised the traditional ballad 'Chevy Chase', but ballads had their main vogue after 1765 when Bishop Percy published his influential *Reliques of Ancient English Poetry*; in this work he frequently edited his old texts to heighten emotional effect and it was these heightened ballads that were often most admired as authentic poetry by his readers.

The most spectacular attempts at finding spontaneous primitive poetry and at aligning the past with the sentimental present were the frauds perpetrated by Thomas Chatterton and James Macpherson. Chatterton, Wordsworth's 'marvellous Boy', seemingly the very type of the sentimental doomed poet, was a self-conscious provincial and bourgeois writer, concerned to intrude the poetry of a specifically British past into the dominant internationalist culture, while James Macpherson was just as eager for the Scottish Gaelic voice he ventriloquized to be heard in the metropolis. But, more than Chatterton, Macpherson drew sentimental attitudes into his creation of the past; his poets and warriors are men of feeling and the Celtic twilight in which they moved easily becomes the less localized sentimental dusk of the graveyard poets.

The characters of *Ossian* are simple, like those in ballads and in much sentimental drama. They are good or bad; the men are valiant and strong, the women beautiful or tearful. The poet who remembers and recreates them is lonely, isolated and sorrowing in heart – tears run down his aged cheeks – and his poetry, like that of Gray and Young among the tombs, is elegiac and grave-ridden:

> 'Sightless I sit by thy tomb. I hear the wind in the wood; but no more I hear my friends. The cry of the hunter is over. The voice of war is ceased.'[8]

Macpherson's tale is of death and the gloomy fascination with death in a dreary landscape, and he is untroubled by the doctrines of Christianity which sit uneasily with the pleasing melancholia of sentimentalism.

Ossian's nature contributes to the melancholy mood. It is made up of dark and howling rivers, mountain streams, sounding rocks, hills of winds and nodding rushes, in an atmosphere of grey flying mist, rising clouds and roaring winds. This generalized nature corresponds with and expresses the human story. It is brought into the foreground when described through Macpherson's use of simple declarative sentences: 'The wind is heard on the mountain. The torrent shrieks down the rock.'

The form of *Ossian* suited the needs of sensibility. To those who believed them genuine, the poems seemed to indicate the authenticity of the apostrophic and elegiac verse of Young and Gray, which no doubt influenced them. Macpherson called his first poetic publication *Fragments* (1760); to the eighteenth-century reader, the short discrete passages in this volume suggested artlessness and a direct recording of evanescent emotions. The style too was indicative of feeling, a kind of 'measured prose' with parallelism of structure as its governing principle; such parallelism was seen by Bishop Lowth as the basic technique of biblical verse.

Macpherson's *Ossian* was part of the literary consciousness of the age; Werther read it to his beloved before he killed himself. The work became the very proof of poetry's invariable and proper connection with emotion and spontaneity, and Hugh Blair extolled it as the 'Poetry of the Heart'.[9] William Duff enthusiastically welcomed the fragments as proof of his theory of the sublime while, on first reading them, Gray was 'so struck, so *extasié* with their infinite beauty' that it seemed unimportant whether or not they were forgeries. Even when by 1819 the imposture was clear, *Ossian* was, according to Hazlitt, 'a feeling and a name that can never be destroyed in the minds of his readers'. Proof that it was 'nothing' would be 'another void left in the heart'.[10]

Women's poetry

The cult of sensibility was a most suitable development for poetical women who could express themselves with perfect propriety in its conventional diction and could exalt their own sensibility without appearing improperly self-centred. Women wrote feelingly on the slave trade and imprisonment, on the poor, on war victims and on the depressed and repressed. Poems abounded with titles such as 'On seeing an Officer's Widow distracted, who had been driven to Despair by a long and fruitless Solicitation for the Arrears of her Pension'. Helen Maria Williams used the association of women and sensibility to feminize both victims and virtues; *Peru* (1784), a poem of protest against war and colonialism, focuses on the women who are excluded from battle but who 'soften Woe' with female tears. Peru becomes an appealing feminine victim and its land- and seascape a kind of desecrated female body: 'the soft waves languid sigh,/ As the lone shore they touch, recede – and die'. In this and in other women's poems the social ills of war, slavery and poverty were opposed simply by social affection, and endings presented tearful tableaux of dying or uniting men and women, bonded by familial sentiment.

On the whole female poets avoided the aggrandizing self-consciousness of the male poets; they rarely assumed the stance of the suffering artist or praised the tradition of despised poetic worth. Instead they wrote much of the physical manifestations of sensibility noted within themselves, their own tremblings, palpitations, blushes and tears, which proved the sentimental worth of the sufferer as well as forming a proper sentimental subject.

As the century wore on, poets worried increasingly about the value of sensibility itself; on the one hand it tended to turn from actual misery, while on the other it implied exquisite marital unhappiness and physical pain. The implication of misery in sensibility was a particular concern of women since, by the late eighteenth century, their perceived identity was inseparable from the quality.

Frances Greville's 'A Prayer for Indifference', probably composed in the 1750s, is a plea to be relieved of sensibility, arguing that its cultivation in women has produced more suffering than joy:

> Nor ease nor peace that heart can know,
>   That, like the needle true,
> Turns at the touch of joy or woe,
>   But, turning, trembles too.
>
> Far as distress the soul can wound,
>   'Tis pain in each degree;
> Bliss goes but to a certain bound,
>   Beyond is agony.

Sensibility exaggerates pain, which has degrees beyond joy; the more sensitive the nerves, the more easily they can be shattered. To endure the life of a woman, fraught as it is with inescapable misery, Greville begs to be relieved of her cultivated sensibility and receive instead sobriety and indifference.

But sensibility would not easily be routed in mid-century and it would be many years before Greville's views would become more than affectation. In the 1750s and 1760s her popular poem did not seem a questioning of sensibility's worth or even a genuine uneasiness at its connection with femininity, but simply an elegant expression of the very quality it decried.

By the last decades of the century, as the tide began to turn against a sensibility which was judged effeminate, destabilizing,

marginally provincial and detrimental to Christian precepts,
feminine sensibility, when embraced, often had a decadent quality
about it, a self-indulgent physicality and a self-contemplating
vanity. The aesthetic experience obscured the ethical, and emotion,
severed from any kind of rationality or action, degenerated into
impulse and sensation.

Helen Maria Williams's 'To Sensibility', published in *Poems*
(1786), avoids even the stylized humanitarianism of her *Peru*.
Taking issue with Frances Greville's apparent questioning of the
gift of a susceptible soul, it asserts the absolute value of sensibility:

> No cold exemption from her pain
> > I ever wish'd to know;
> Cheer'd with her transport, I sustain
> > Without complaint or woe.

Sensibility, inevitably a female figure, causes 'every finer bliss' and
'lights the melting eye/With looks to anguish dear'. Clearly it is the
mercurial responsiveness that is valued, not its benevolent power
over the external world, which Shaftesbury had found so 'manly',
or even its gift of virtuous pleasure:

> Quick, as the trembling metal flies,
> > When heat or cold impels,
> Her anxious heart to joy can rise,
> > Or sink where anguish dwells.

The 'sacred power to weep' is a good in itself, regardless of cause.

Literary feminine sensibility of the sort Helen Maria Williams
conveys here differs from the sensibility of the male poet who
retreats from the crude world to open himself to poetic inspiration.
Even such passive creativity seems too active for the lady poet
who, however, cannot easily adopt the posture of distress, often
dependent on sexual failing, conveyed in the fiction of the time,
although some erotically charged distress certainly adds lustre to
her image. The octet of a typical poem on Williams, entitled
'Sonnet, on seeing Miss Helen Maria Williams weep at a Tale of
Distress', illustrates this point, for it delivers the sentimental female
poet as object of male contemplation, removed from any creative
power:

> She wept. – Life's purple tide began to flow
> In languid streams through every thrilling vein;

Dim were my swimming eyes – my pulse beat slow,
And my full heart was swell'd to dear delicious pain.
Life left my loaded heart, and closing eye;
A sigh recall'd the wanderer to my breast;
Dear was the pause of life, and dear the sigh
That call'd the wanderer home, and home to rest.

This poem is William Wordsworth's first published achievement and it typifies the occasional verse in the magazines of the 1780s. The poet did not actually see Helen Maria Williams cry – he was not to meet her until many years later when his style of writing and her style of living had much changed (she supported the French Revolution and was denounced in England as an 'unsex'd female'). In the sonnet, however, Wordsworth has constructed his subject as the deliciously distressed and distressing lady, whose literary tears implied no other activity in her beyond crying, not even writing, although it was her reputation as an emotional feminine poet that initially prompted this recreation. Her tears which proclaim 'each virtue in her' merely provoke further tears in the sensitive man. The subject here is sensation itself, indiscriminate and common but not actually shared; it is enervated, morbid and supremely self-obsessed.

It was this kind of sensibility that disturbed Hannah More, a lady synonymous in later life with a moral conservative commonsensical stance, but the author in 1782 of a poem entitled 'Sensibility: To Mrs Boscawen'. In a manner reminiscent of Helen Maria Williams, the work openly addresses itself to Frances Greville's point, that sensibility tends to exacerbate the misery of the sensitive person; more covertly, however, it manifests an uneasiness at the solipsistic, sentimental postures revealed by Williams and Wordsworth, the sentimentalist's habit of turning from misery to contemplate his or her own sensations.

To Greville's perception that 'the feeling heart/ Shapes its own wound', Hannah More makes the snobbish response that none the less it is better to be with the sentimental élite than with the unfeeling vulgar. Those 'who ne'er a pain but for themselves have known' are unimaginative and dull company; they call 'romantic ev'ry finer thought/ Conceiv'd by pity, or by friendship wrought'. Like Williams, More reiterated the sentimentalist's claim that troubled Greville, that intense misery must be felt by those capable of intense joy, since the capacity for one implies capacity for the other: 'Would you, to 'scape the pain, the joy forego,/ And miss the transport to avoid the woe?' Finally she argues that sorrow to the sentimental person may be enjoyable; remembered woe is 'not unpleasing sadness' and 'tender Sorrow has her pleasures too', and she accepts with equanimity that 'Where glow exalted sense and taste refin'd,/ There keener anguish rankles in the mind'.

Hannah More has greater trouble over the sentimentalist's habit of turning from misery to contemplate his or her own suffering. Thus, although in orthodox sentimental fashion she defines her subject as divine ('this quick'ning spark of Deity'), innate ('Thou hasty moral! sudden sense of right!') and spontaneous (benevolence 'seldom stays to chuse' and sentimental friendship 'once deter-min'd, never swerves'), she is very much aware of developments since Shaftesbury hailed benevolent joy and moral beauty, and she is eager to defend sensibility against charges of physical self-indulgence. True sensibility, she insists, is not the artificial ecstasy or elegant mourning at a sparrow's fall; it is not a selfish literary mode, although notably she originates her own love of virtue in Richardson's novels. Instead it is active compassion, patient love and forbearance in irritating and painful situations.

In Hannah More's division of proper and improper sensibility, the collapse of sensibility as a poetic mode is foreshadowed. Once the physical response, the aesthetics of suffering and the sensational aspects of emotion such as Helen Maria Williams caught are publicly divorced from, for example, pity, patience and tolerance, which are yet asserted, a straightforward Christian ethic appears and it becomes unnecessary and inappropriate to extol sensibility. When More sneers at those who scorn life's duties to cry at fiction and who relieve suffering 'cheaply – with a tear', she is progressing out of sensibility altogether. A mark of her growing insecurity is her interruption of her own flow of enthusiasm for sympathy, benevolence and friendship to mourn, in the triumph of sensibility, the unsentimental 'manly' virtues of heroic justice and stern truth.

V   *Fiction: Samuel Richardson*

The early proto-novel of the seventeenth century and the first decades of the eighteenth lived in a variety of breathless, quick-moving forms: rogue histories and whore biographies for example, marvellous travel tales, scandal chronicles and romantic novellas. Although many of these forms had schematic morality and stylized conflicts of gender and ideology, sentimental fiction was descended most obviously from two particular types. The first, the sensational and titillating scandalous tale of writers such as Delarivière Manley and Eliza Haywood, pits female innocence and sensitivity against aristocratic male libertinage and economic power; it is artificial and mannered in style, euphemistically treating complex issues of sexual desire, seduction and rape within an already conventional plot of love intrigue leading to marriage and death. The second type of fiction, written by more publicly virtuous authors than either Haywood or Manley, is cautionary, didactic and unerotic, close in aim to the exemplary tales and anecdotes of Addison and Steele in the *Tatler* and the *Spectator*; it can range from stern and simple warnings about marital disobedience to Jane Barker's psychologically disturbing stories of marital avoidance.[1]

From both types of fiction – the scandal narrative and the

cautionary tale – the sentimental novel took elements: the overcharged, unrealistic and expressive style, the severe didactic aim, and the stress on virtue in the heroine and (often) in the writer. But on the whole the sentimental novel moved away from those elements of early fiction that seemed to foreshadow the realistic novel: the open treatment of erotic and psychological complexities, occasionally manifest in the cautionary and scandalous tales, for example, or the social ambiguities caught in the rogue narratives of Defoe.

Samuel Richardson is clearly the most important figure in early sentimental fiction, for in the mid-eighteenth century his novels made the new form serious and respectable. Taking the schematic story of 'faithless Men, and ruin'd Maids' in Eliza Haywood's memorable phrase, Richardson used the epistolary form to investigate the key problems and concepts of sentimentalism: the expression and moral implications of sensibility and the ideal of benevolence and social harmony. In addition he made the sentimental construction of woman a dominant motif and the minute recordings of emotional and physical states a central purpose.

Richardson's novels generated an immense quantity of European and British literature – 'an infinite series of other compositions' according to the hostile *Critical Remarks on Sir Charles Grandison, Clarissa and Pamela* (1754) – which took the Richardsonian themes and conventions as the basis and precondition of its art, while their situations and schemes entered the culture as almost mythic events. The French author Madame de Staël felt Clarissa's escape from her father's house as an action within her own childhood, and many other real and constructed people lived out the emotions and stances of Richardson's embattled heroines. A host of men and women writers rehearsed the comic *Pamela* and tragic *Clarissa* plots using versions of the Richardsonian style; several generations of young girls wrote to their bosom friends in this sentimental mode and prided themselves on the sensitivity Pamela had taught them physically and verbally to display. Given the centrality of Richardson, F. R. Leavis's assertion in *The Great Tradition*, that he would never again be a current classic, would have mightily astonished the eighteenth century.

At first, Richardson seems an unlikely candidate for the mythic enterprise his novels represent. He began life modestly as an apprentice printer in London and through economic astuteness and literary acumen worked his way into the middle reaches of the bourgeoisie. Yet there are many factors within his prudent life that argue his suitability as the spokesman of the new philosophy of sentiment.

First, although in his prosperous days his friends were often from the gentry and although in his humblest days he seems a member of the lowest orders, Richardson was for much of his life clearly associated with the middle class. This was the class to which the denigrators of sentimentalism assigned its beliefs and art. Second, Richardson's lack of the classical education felt necessary for gentlemen aligned him with women of any class, since they were similarly deprived, and woman's consciousness became predominantly the place of sensibility. Third, Richardson's class position connected success and prosperity to work and self-assessment. This in turn tied him to the Dissenters and their emphasis on moral self-help and self-knowledge; their scrutinizing of thought and activity in journals and autobiographies foreshadows the soul-searchings and self-reliance of the fictional creations.[2]

Richardson, then, represents a powerful coalescence of trends and interests. While catching something of the individualism of the economically expansive men of the middle class, he also expresses both the domestic-communal concerns of women who have little part in this expansion, and the conduct-book ethics of the old Puritan tradition. His extraordinary influence must undoubtedly be due in part to his representativeness, as well as to his immense originality.

The novels

Richardson's three novels – *Pamela* (1740–1), *Clarissa* (1747–8) and *Sir Charles Grandison* (1753–4) – are in conversation with each other over sensibility and virtue. *Pamela* tells of a servant girl far from her poor but honest parents who on the death of her mistress is subjected to the sexual pursuit of Mr B, her young master.[3] She both dampens and enflames him with a display of virtuous sensibility that heightens her charms and that goes far beyond the capabilities of ladies of higher social status. The pursuit is frenzied, but Mr B is always checked by Pamela's frightened passivity and he fears her death in her many faintings and fits. To further his purpose and separate her from her admiring supporters, he removes her to another of his houses, where she is placed under the charge of the wickedly masculine Mrs Jewkes, who counsels her master speedily to prosecute his will. Pamela despairs almost to suicide, until Mr B, tired of the game, sends her homewards. By this time, despite – or some might say because of – his atrocious treatment, Pamela realizes that she has lost her 'heart' to her master. Thus, when he asks her to return of her own free will, she does so, and he marries her. She deserves this social elevation because of her unceasing emotional, spiritual and physical superiority. Her odyssey, recounted in letters and journals, is displayed for her master, his sister, her parents and the neighbouring gentry, who are all moved to tears of admiration and affection at so matchless a lady.

The second part of *Pamela* follows the heroine into exemplary wifehood. She is found reforming all who come close to her and teaching them how to promote piety and harmony in households without unsettling the hierarchy. She withstands the temptation to oppose the 'male prerogative' and she urges Mr B back from an extramarital affair with a dashing widow by her mingling of frankness and submission. She ends as the mother of numerous children fulfilling all female social roles of wife, friend, neighbour, mother and mistress.

Richardson must have felt that there remained something vulgar about virtue's complete reward in this world and something difficult to stomach in the picture of domestic bliss Pamela illustrates, predicated as it is on the fragile conversion of Mr B's lust. In *Clarissa,* his next novel, which he describes as 'a much nobler and more useful Story than that of Pamela', the struggle of feminine virtue and male sexuality is not so easily resolved, but instead continues to death.[4] Meanwhile the doctrines of sentimentalism, too neatly exemplified in *Pamela*, are tested until they reveal their harsh implications and limits.

Clarissa is the story of a virtuous woman trapped in an ambitious and avaricious family, dominated by a choleric father, a spiteful sister and a bullying brother. In keeping with the tendency of the age, the aim of the Harlowe family is the aggrandisement and elevation of the eldest son; thus the grandfather's legacy of some property to Clarissa herself is seen as contradictory to this end. Against the wishes of her close friend and confidante, the spirited Anna Howe, but in accordance with her own pious views of filial duty, Clarissa immediately gives up the management of the estate to her father.

But she is marked for the family's spite none the less and, when the attractive but morally corrupt aristocrat Lovelace pays court to Clarissa, the Harlowes combine to force her into an odious and repulsive match. Immense pressures and outright cruelty persuade her to accept the protection of Lovelace, and she escapes with him from what she apprehends as a forced marriage.

The seeming elopement to which Clarissa ultimately did not assent has long been plotted. Once out of her father's house, Clarissa is a prey to all the manic strategies of Lovelace, who sees her virtuous independence as a demand for cruelty and violation. Using whores to impersonate his relatives, he lures her into a brothel where she is mocked and reviled but remains unsubdued. Finally, urged by the women of the house, he drugs and rapes her. As he says, he 'can go no further'.

Although morally intact, Clarissa feels the rape as a blow to her identity, for the ideology of the time made sexuality an act of possession and she is, as Lovelace believes, now his. After a brief madness, she escapes and prepares to die. Her lengthy death – not suicide but certainly willed and aided by her refusal to eat – is witnessed by a tearful host of the moderately good. After her death her desire that peace should be re-established is ignored when her cousin Morden returns to kill Lovelace.

Clarissa became the absolute example of the virtuous woman. Could there be a male equivalent? Richardson tried to answer this question in his final novel *Sir Charles Grandison*, the story of the 'good MAN', and his very public difficulties are evident. He discussed his lack of plot and character motivation with many of his female correspondents and admitted his fear of creating 'a *faultless* monster' (*Correspondence*, III, p. 168)[5].

While there remains in this book some force in the female characters who are the central correspondents – in their plots of suffering, madness and attempted rape and in the pert or submissive responses to male social power – the hero Sir Charles Grandison has very little to do but extricate himself with honour from one lady, the foreign Clementina, and bestow himself on another, the English Harriet. Since he is a man of power, his sensibility and virtue are not in opposition to society but combined with it; there is therefore essentially no story and Richardson is caught in the narrative problem, adumbrated by Steele in *The Christian Hero* (1701) of how to keep together the heroic social qualities and Christian sensibility.

Sir Charles's character cannot be tested, only announced; one might argue that he exists mainly as a construct of the main female characters who seem to live only to write letters about him and who rapturously extol him as goodness in a '*manly* heart', as 'The Christian: The Hero', as 'an imitator of the Almighty', as indeed 'every-thing'. (An Italian bishop declares that were he a Catholic he 'might expect canonization'.) It is only a pity, as Richardson himself appears to have felt, that English laws prevented Grandison from making more than one lady perfectly happy.

Instruction

Richardson never tired of stressing the instructional aim of literature – in letters, in prefaces, in postscripts to novels and in critical passages. For instance he praised *The London Merchant* because it was the only work of early eighteenth-century drama to provide an example to the youth of the city. When Prévost, Richardson's translator, complained of the sacrifice of story to morality in the novels, Richardson declared that the morality was 'the very motive with me, of the story's being written at all'. Instruction was so widely accepted an aim that it was expressed not only by Richardson but also by his detractor – the anonymous 'Lover of Virtue' – in *Critical Remarks*, who roundly asserted: 'It is, no doubt, the indispensable duty of every writer to promote, as far as lies in his power . . . the advancement of virtue, especially the moral and social duties of mutual good-will and universal benevolence' (p. 7). Diderot affirmed that Richardson's fiction had softened his heart and compelled him to choose oppressed virtue over triumphant vice.

As an instructor through literature Richardson began with *Letters written to and for Particular Friends, on the Most Important Occasions*, which taught people of the lower orders how to express moral opinions and feeling response; proper expression and exemplary stances came together. Out of this work grew *Pamela*, a novel which Richardson hoped 'might tend to promote the cause of religion and virtue' by providing examples of parental, filial and social duties and by giving guidance to virgins, brides and wives.

The title page of *Pamela I* states the aim succinctly: the book's purpose is 'to cultivate the Principles of Virtue and Religion in the Minds of the Youth of Both Sexes'. The method is described in the Preface: improvement will come through contemplation of virtue made lovely. After the success of the first part of *Pamela*,

Richardson added a second to reveal the good woman in her domestic responses and to show, in one character's words, 'what every body may do' but which is 'yet so beautiful, so laudable, so uncommon in the practice . . .' (II. p. 179). Rules were provided for general conduct 'in a genteel and useful Married Life' and the novel ends with almost allegorical cautionary tales invented by Pamela to instruct young ladies in the route of virtue.

Referring to the popular religious conduct-book, *The Whole Duty of Man*, Edward Young called *Clarissa* 'the Whole Duty of a Woman'. Richardson was clear that he intended his novel 'for an Example' or, as he explained in a letter of 1746/7, 'I would not have set Pen to Paper'.[6] Anna Howe and Clarissa, 'young Ladies of virtue and honour' and two of the main correspondents of the book, were to display 'a practical friendship, that demonstrates virtue, delicacy, impartiality', and the novel ends with an account from Anna of Clarissa's early life as an exemplary pattern for young ladies, who are taught to rise early, regulate their time, and engage in judicious charity. The exemplary account comes close to early conduct-books of practical goodness and is quite distinct from the kind of dramatic and intensely varied action presented in the harsh central conflict.

Richardson declared that his aim in *Clarissa* was cautionary as well as exemplary – the book was written 'for the sake of *Example* and *Warning*' – to show 'the distresses that may attend the misconduct both of parents and children in relation to marriage' and, like *Pamela*, it encloses cautionary tales of misguided women. The author of *Critical Remarks*, seeking to find whether the novels 'have a Tendency to corrupt or improve the Public Taste and Morals', judged this cautionary aim successful: 'if the morals contained in your Clarissa, had their due weight, a vast variety of mischiefs and miseries in private life would be prevented' (p. 8).

The Preface to *Sir Charles Grandison* rehearses Richardson's fictional efforts, arguing that *Pamela* had revealed the 'Superiority of Virtue' and the contemptible character of the 'Libertine'; *Clarissa*, exemplary of 'a truly *Christian Heroine*', had been a 'Warning to Parents' against tyrannizing over children and a caution to 'the gay Part of Mankind' against that 'Misuse of Wit and Youth, of Rank and Fortune, and of every outward Accomplishment, which turns them into a Curse to the miserable Possessor, as well as to all around him'. The new book was exemplary of 'a Man of TRUE HONOUR', a 'Man of Religion and Virtue; of Liveliness and Spirit; accomplished and agreeable; happy in himself, and a Blessing to others'. *Sir Charles Grandison* was not 'published ultimately, nor even principally, any more than the other two, for the Sake of Entertainment only'.

Sir Charles enters as exemplary and is given the kind of sententious remarks that playwrights addressed to their audiences through the protagonists of sentimental drama: 'Vice is the greatest coward in the world, when it knows it will be resolutely oppos'd' for example. Meanwhile the lives of minor characters, such as the servant who 'fell into a bad service' or the gay dissolute father of Sir Charles, form straight cautionary tales familiar from *Pamela* and *Clarissa*. Since, according to Richardson, major characters should be drawn in such a way as to illustrate exemplary traits, these should be announced before and after their exponents appear. Sir Charles in particular is constructed as exemplary before he even opens his mouth and his display of virtue is strenuously supported by the praise and approbation of onlookers.

Clearly Richardson went to extraordinary lengths to make his instructive aim manifest within all three novels. In addition, major ideas of *Clarissa* were repeated in tables of contents placed at the end of each volume so that readers could recapitulate the instruction of the story, while a postscript justifies the heroine's conduct. In 1755 he went further by detaching his sentiments and moral generalizations from his stories and publishing them separately as *A Collection of Moral and Instructive Sentiments, Maxims, Cautions and Reflexions, Contained . . . in The Histories of Pamela, Clarissa and Sir Charles Grandison*; the work should, he hoped, ease instruction and prove that his fiction had ignored few articles of conduct.[7]

Richardson's moral and pedagogic aim is quite clear, then, but his methods are more problematic. There is, to begin with, the plot that must yield instruction. Samuel Johnson remarked that if one read Richardson for the story one risked hanging oneself with impatience, and listeners have testified to their ability to sleep through parts of *Sir Charles Grandison* and wake without having lost any important elements of action.

And yet the Richardsonian plots have considerable life, not always clearly directed at instruction. Having read *Pamela*, Henry Fielding turned its plot into the mocking *Shamela*, the story of a maid no better than she should be who traps a master into marriage through a display of sex-invested sensibility; the author of *Pamela Censured: in a Letter to the Editor* (1741) provides the following subtitle for his attack: 'Shewing That under the Specious Pretence of Cultivating the Principles of Virtue in the Minds of the Youth of both Sexes, the MOST ARTFUL and ALLURING AMOROUS IDEAS are convey'd.' A young male reader must, the critic asserts, wish to try out Mr B's methods himself, while a young female will imagine her own breasts fondled and either prepare for seduction or 'privately . . . seek Remedies which may drive her to the most unnatural Excesses'.

The plot of *Clarissa* is more subtly problematic, for it shows that virtue, to display itself in fiction, requires a context of hostility and aggression. Many readers of the early parts begged the author to avoid an unhappy ending, and in his replies Richardson revealed the dependence on Christianity of his version of literary sentimentalism, and the necessity of reparation in the next world for unalloyed misery in this. In fact he declared that the need for the Christian scheme, shown by the plot of tortured innocence, made it superior to the tragic plan of poetical justice, where a great protagonist fell because of a flaw or sin. The delay in the extrication of 'suffering Virtue' on earth, which provoked the outcry from susceptible readers and which makes the novel painfully compelling, would in Richardson's opinion be intolerable without the acceptance of its heavenly reward; yet to extricate it on earth in the face of Christian revelation would be an affront to faith. It was, then, only readers and future writers without Richardson's Christian beliefs who could find and make the *Clarissa* plot sensational. *Clarissa* was, Richardson asserted, a 'Religious Novel'; it was 'not to be considered as a *mere Amusement* . . . but . . . intended to inculcate the HIGHEST and *most* IMPORTANT *Doctrines*'.

In a letter justifying the sad ending of *Clarissa* to those who, despite all Christian assurances, yearned for a fairy-tale conclusion of married bliss, Richardson revealed how thoroughly he seems to have felt the sentimental novel both as an expression of the Christian scheme and as an escape from reality and fictional realism. 'Happiness' in the real world has no clarity, he wrote; it exists only by comparison and it grows stagnant if it lasts long. Even the seemingly happiest looked forward to what they hadn't got. And what, he asked, does even the 'happy' life of a real woman consist in? A round of pregnancies, child rearing and domestic duties. Surely Christian death might be preferable (*Selected Letters*, pp. 106–7). (Incidentally, if any proof were required for the notion that the sentimental novel intentionally eschewed realism, this comment might well provide it.)

The problem of *Grandison's* plot was rather different, since there is no fear of the worldly interpretations of *Pamela* and *Clarissa* or of the sensationalizing of virtue's distress. Sir Charles is, as is often reiterated, all goodness, but it is goodness coupled not with sentimental female helplessness, even though 'his is the gentlest of manly minds', but with male power. 'Your good man will be out of nature, if he is not persecuted', remarked a correspondent to Richardson during the writing (*Correspondence, V*, p. 210). Yet no one can persecute a man whose tongue, arm and influence are all-powerful, although Richardson tries to moderate the invulner-ability of his hero by placing him in Catholic aristrocratic Italy where his lineage and status are less admired and his manners not immediately overwhelming. But in England Sir Charles arrives perfect and his sisters' slight show of imperfect spirit subsides in his presence into trickling tears and the irresistible desire to kiss his hand. As Harriet truly remarks, 'There is no living within the blazing glory of this man!' Since goodness in the person of the hero is not poor or on the run from society – on the contrary he has 'so much power, and such a will to do us good' – no one need die and even Clementina, the lady who loses the prize, seems saved for a lesser marriage.

Like the plot, Richardson's characters also pose problems when they are read straightforwardly for instruction. Pamela might, for example, be found repellently narcissistic, far too concerned with her own ruffled appearance, while the author of the *Critical Remarks* on Richardson found Clarissa 'rather too good, at least too methodically so'. Sir Charles was 'an inconsistent angel', totally unsuitable for imitation and Richardson had to justify at length his possession of the female virtues of modesty and chastity. Lady Mary Wortley Montagu considered all the exemplary characters of *Grandison* ridiculously candid and prolix. She complained in particular of the main correspondent, Harriet Byron: 'in this Mortal state of Imperfection Fig leaves are as necessary for our Minds as our Bodies, and tis as indecent to shew all we think as all we have.'[8]

Sentimental exemplary response is, however, not simply a matter of following a plot or copying a character's actions. Rather it is attention to the sentiment of the work. Richardson wanted to be read 'for the sentiment', considering, as Johnson declared after his exasperated comment on the Richardsonian plot, 'the story as only giving occasion for the sentiment'.[9] Characters should teach through their gestures and responses as well as their deeds and verbal expressions. Since the actual situation of the heroines is often extreme and since the characters displayed are indeed almost perfect and necessarily self-regarding, they came closest to the reader not in activity and personality but in their displays of emotion. The reader should be moved less by identification with the characters – a process Richardson, like many other sentimental writers, seems to have feared – than by contemplation of these emotional displays. Feeling created in and by the novel should be sentimentally contagious.

Richardson accepted the sentimental theory that moral improvement derived from pity. So in a letter he tells of his aim to 'soften and mend the Heart'. Since virtue could be generated through an exciting to compassion, that reader would be most improved who had been most deeply affected. The supreme spectacle was innocence wronged, virtue in distress. Clarissa was, then, beyond any psychological complexity, to be 'a true Object of Pathos'. Such pathos would provoke compassion and nurture fortitude: 'My Story is designed to strengthen the tender Mind, and to enable the worthy Heart to bear up against the Calamities of Life' (*Selected Letters*, p. 111). As in his remarks on plot, Richardson here again insisted on the Christian element in his depiction in *Clarissa* of utter innocence and utter distress: originally he had, he declared, 'intended to make her so faultless, that a Reader should find no way to account for the Calamities she met with, and to justify Moral Equity, but by looking up to a future Reward' (*Selected Letters*. p. 73).

Despite his insistence on instruction and Christian expression in fiction, Richardson, like his readers, well knew the power of the novel to escape from stated aims and pious intentions. In the early years of the form there was uneasiness at fiction's ability to overwhelm the reader's mind and considerable fear that it was a dubious instrument of improvement. Its fantasy was felt to conquer reality and seduce against the admonitions of morality. Understanding this possibility, Richardson made strenuous efforts to control the meaning of his texts, to force the reader into the single reading he wanted by constantly tinkering with his edition – the fact that he served as his own printer made this especially easy for him. *Clarissa* in particular provoked what Richardson regarded as misinterpretation and he twice told the story of reading the characterization and fate of Lovelace to 'a young Lady of seventeen', who, to his annoyance, pitied his villain. Richardson returned to his text to make Lovelace 'still more and more odious, by his heighten'd Arrogance and Triumph' (*Selected Letters*, pp. 73, 113). Between the first draft in 1744 and the third edition in 1751 much other rewriting, omitting and restoring occurred in response to readers' reactions, with the stated aim of rendering the psychological drama clearer, cruder and more schematic, of enhancing the delicacy of Clarissa and blackening the villainy of Lovelace. Footnotes were added to nudge readers into responsible sentimental response.

Even worse than a reader's possible misreading was a writer's theft and misappropriation of his texts. In the novels the women's letters in particular have their own integrity; this is frequently violated by men who stealthily take possession of and sully these letters in a way that expresses the seduction or rape they purpose. When Richardson heard of a debased continuation of his own *Pamela* before he himself had concluded it, he felt like the father of an abused daughter; his plan had been 'Ravished out of my Hands, and, probably my Characters depreciated and debased, by those who knew nothing of the Story, nor the Delicacy required in the Continuation of the Piece' (*Selected Letters*, p. 43).

Richardson insisted that in his novels he had everywhere avoided 'inflaming Descriptions, even when Rake writes to Rake' (*Selected Letters*, p. 105). None the less he must in some fashion have accepted his fictional force and the voyeurism he inevitably allowed his readers, for there is in the novels, along with the crude manipulation of footnotes, an effort to defuse the power of 'inflaming': through the curious repetition and modification of scenes that might be judged most titillating. An example from *Pamela* occurs when Mr B in his house in Lincolnshire makes a scene of sexual theatre with his prisoner on show and with himself and Mrs Jewkes as onlookers.[10]

Mr B both humiliates and reifies Pamela when she is forced to wait on him at table and, in spite of her grief, pour his wine and stand to reflect her charms in his glass. During the scene she lies on the floor, sobs and weeps and is spurned and reviled by Mr B, who at the same time extols her physical attractions: 'what a shape! what a neck! what a hand!' he exclaims. It is a performance with decided sado–masochistic content and it is reflected, as in a kind of overhead mirror, in the letters Pamela writes to describe it; these are later read avidly by Mr B. Much further on in the novel, the scene of humiliation and aggression is repeated, with Lady Davers substituting for Mr B and trying the same haughty tricks. Again Pamela is commanded to wait at table, she is taunted, and her image in the mirror is commented on. But the second scene is without the sexual threat of the earlier, for only the feeble nephew provides a male presence, and Pamela is by this time invulnerable, since she is safely a wife. Where the first scene was charged with sexuality, the second is desexualized, so much so that it can be converted from private sexual to public social entertainment. The scene is described in letters of course, but it is also verbally displayed for Mr B and friends who, the reader learns, are sentimentally improved by it.

Sentimental signs

'A feeling heart is a blessing that no one, who has it, would be without; and it is a moral security of innocence; since the heart that is able to partake of the distress of another, cannot wilfully give it', wrote Richardson in *Sir Charles Grandison*. In the world of this fiction, tears indicate correct response; they denote tenderness, sympathy and a feeling heart. The good characters react to suffering with subtle gradations from weeping hysterically to dropping a single tear. Such physical manifestations constitute a language of the heart, a code of sincere and true expression far beyond words which have the ability to lie and conceal. Much can be forgiven if the heart is right, the premise also of Fielding's *Tom Jones*. Mr B may plot and scheme for most of volume I, but his sudden and little-motivated reformation will be real when it comes because 'his heart is naturally beneficent'.

Failure to reform, like reformation, is a physical display. In *Clarissa*, the heroine's antithesis, the wicked Sinclair, is startlingly ugly and hardhearted, and her repulsive and noisy death of mortification contrasts with the purifying, emaciating and quiet death of Clarissa:

> she was raving, crying, cursing, and even howling, more like a wolf than a human creature . . . Behold her, then, spreading the whole tumbled bed with her huge quaggy carcass . . . her matted

grizzly hair, made irreverent by her wickedness . . . spread about her fat ears and brawny neck . . . her bellows-shaped and various-coloured breasts ascending by turns to her chin, and descending out of sight, with the violence of her gaspings. (IV, pp. 380–2)

She is surrounded in her dying by her obscene, dishevelled and foul-smelling 'daughters'. The author of *Critical Remarks*, who is firmly on the side of verisimilitude in fiction and out of sympathy with Richardson's meaningful physical scheme, finds the connection of prostitution and physical decay quite absurd because untrue to life where whores are, he notes, usually very careful of their persons.

In physical expressiveness women are pre-eminent in the novels. Men may be susceptible, as Richardson shows in his correspondence when he described himself completely shaken by a reading: 'I found, in short, such Tremors, such Startings that I was unable to go thro' it.' Richardson wishes a cure for this inconvenient susceptibility in himself, but, when he speaks to his friend Lady Bradshaigh about a similar sensitivity in her, he finds her very humanity expressed through it. One reason for this gendering of sensibility is clearly the physical weakness assumed for women. As Harriet Byron declares, 'A man cannot ask for compassion, as a woman can.' Often men will imitate women's sensibility when reduced to their impotence: the erring father of Sir Charles, when he is weak and bedridden from a wound, is overcome by the virtuous dying of his wife, but, when he is strong again, he resumes his wicked ways. A further reason is Richardson's insistence, in direct opposition to La Mettrie's *L'Homme machine*, that sexuality and sensibility are at odds and that the former is threatening to the latter and to individual integrity. Non-sexual sensibility is best exemplified in women for whom chastity is imperative.

Weak, non-sexual women are, then, the supreme exponents of sensibility for Richardson and its signs may be developed in them more intensively than in men. Men wipe their tears and calm themselves by walking to a window or by otherwise concealing their state, and their gestures often remain unprobed. Sir Charles exists mainly as onlookers see and construct him and he does not record the minutiae of feelings in the manner of Pamela, Clarissa or Harriet. It is the watching women not the active hero who most uncontrollably display feelings and who describe and comment on them at overwhelming length.

Since women are so much associated with sensibility, the female body is sincere for Richardson, as for the dramatists of pathos, and its manifestations and gestures true and easy to read: 'a man of common penetration may see to the bottom of a woman's heart', Sir Charles considers. According to Mr B, eyes are the windows of women's souls, glistening with honest emotion and expressing sentiments before their tongues can speak them. Harriet Byron's character can be read in her face, and her 'heart' in her eyes; on learning that Sir Charles is endangered by a duel, Harriet, who has not yet declared herself in love, curtsies, sighs and blushes, and, when she fears he is elsewhere engaged, her upper lip 'quiver'd like as aspen leaf'.

The ability of good women to express themselves authentically and appealingly through physical signs is especially irksome to bad characters. The wicked sister Arabella regards Clarissa's metonymic gestures, her lifted hands and streaming eyes, as 'witchcrafts' and manipulation, while the whores are spurred by these signs to demand her desecration.

Both Harriet and Clarissa respond extremely to the idea of abduction and rape and neither can immediately describe her experience. Pamela and Clarissa convey darkly through allegory and dream what their bodies make quite clear. All the heroines fall into fits, which Harriet continues to suffer even after her safety is assured. Locke argued for knowledge from sensation; the Richardsonian female seems to arrest this progress so that knowledge stays at the level of sensation and the body.

In Clementina of *Sir Charles Grandison*, Richardson shows female sensibility pushed to the extreme of hysteria, and he charts the progress and cure of this disease as outlined in the medical books of Robert James and Dr George Cheyne which he printed. Clementina's madness is feminine and pure, a disorder of refined sensibility. Cruelly treated, she none the less preserved her femininity and was 'all patient, resigned, her hands crossed on her bosom, praying for mercy, not by speech, but by her eyes'; 'even in the height of her malady' she never 'uttered a wish or a thought that was contrary to her duty either to God, or her parents; nor yet to the honour of her name, and . . . the *pride* of her sex'. Her madness is not an overturning of her femininity but an extreme expression of sympathetic sensibility and of the impotence always implied in the concept. Consequently, the words 'noble' and 'delicate' are much used for her while she is insane, and a suitor writes of her, 'I loved Clementina above all women, *before* her illness. I loved her not the less *for* her illness'; 'O what eloquence in her disorder', exclaims Sir Charles.

The extraordinary nature of the Richardsonian equation of woman's body with sensibility is pointed out by the author of *Critical Remarks*, who notes that the conventional physical mani-festations of women which the novelist presents – their palpitations and faintings – would seem extremely odd to people from an entirely different culture (p. 18). Richardson himself would have been astonished had he observed his own literary legacy, in which physical debility in due course became not simply an authentic expression but a kind of seductiveness: 'The feeblenesses to which the tender frame of woman is subject, are, perhaps, more seducing than her bloom . . . in nursing that which *droops* (sweetly dejected) and is ready to fall upon its bed, our care becomes more dear . . . objects are beloved in proportion . . . as they are gentle, unresisting, and pathetic.'[11]

'Woman is the glory of all created existence', exclaims Sir Charles Grandison to Harriet, who responds with a blush and a tremble. Because of its sensibility, the female sex for Richardson bears a large meaning; sensitive women, although always socially subdued, become spiritually privileged and morally superior to lustful and less sensitive men: 'The cause of virtue, and of the sex, can hardly be separated', he wrote in *Grandison*, and Sir Charles declares that good women have more tenderness and sympathy than good men and that their pity is more generous. Following the she-tragedies and female novellas, Richardson definitively for-mulated the myth that made socially subordinate women pure, transparent and redemptive, expressing their superior morality not in action or in intellectual enterprise – 'women's minds have generally a lighter turn than those of men' – but in nice moral discrimination and in the physical signs of sensibility. In his pages femininity became so elevated that a steadfast adherence to innate feminine qualities assured goodness; femininity could hardly coexist with evil at all and, when erring women repented through their reduction to a sentimental display, they usually remained repentant for they had been returned to their proper sentimental character. In so far as women were truly wicked, they simply lacked femininity and acquired masculine traits. When a kept woman in *Grandison* is in a passion, there is not 'a female feature . . . in her face'; Sinclair and Mrs Jewkes are 'masculine' and their wickedness 'unwomanly'. Clarissa speculates that her cruel sister has 'a soul of the *other* Sex in a body of *ours*' (III, p. 216). Throughout the century these terms would be used for female villains or for women who failed in some way to conform to the sentimental construction of femininity.

Pamela and Clarissa struggle with the problem of the significance of virginity and both accept the double standard. There is no doubt that a sexual slip, although not appreciated, is permissible in Mr B, although impossible for Pamela. A good fallen woman, if she has great spirituality, will die; if not, she will repent like Sally Godfrey. A bad woman will become a whore and die a putrid death. But a fallen man may go on, as Mr B does, to become the master of the most virtuous lady and be termed by her the best of men. This double standard, this demand for a higher level of behaviour in women, is referred by Pamela and Clarissa not simply to the greater social power of men but also to the superior morality of the young woman.

Fellowship

Shaftesbury prized benevolence as a harmonizing force in a society and as a pleasurable sensation in the agent. The Richardsonian hero or heroine benefits others, usually with exemplary prudence, and receives rapt gratitude in return. The suffering before benevolence has acted provokes tears in the benefactor, who is in return rewarded by tears of gratitude in the sufferer and is thus confirmed in the resolve for future benevolence. Benevolence acts through sympathy which creates, as Shaftesbury and Hume argued, an ideal society, distinct from and opposed to the Hobbesian huddle of frightened men. In his three novels Richardson tries to portray fictionally the sentimental fellowship of benevolence and sympathy.

The ideal grouping of *Pamela* and *Grandison* is a kind of feudal, golden-age one, with beneficent master or mistress ruling for its own good a community of servants and children. The deeply inegalitarian society is presented in familial terms, so that the pressures and tensions that might be disruptive are contained by parental and fraternal images. In Richardson's novels, servants and tenants are like brothers, mothers, fathers or, most often, children, and the never-ending dependence of their situation is hidden in the heady delights of relationship.

In the opening pages of the second volume of *Pamela*, the feudal image of sentimental fellowship is confirmed by both houses of Mr B: his own and the one lent to Pamela's parents. Good stewardship is mentioned as a desirable quality in old Andrews, but, apart from this, there is little suggestion of the economic basis of the communities. All is non-exploitative and pastoral; even the 'kine' come 'lowing and crowding' round the old couple. In this society the good are rewarded with money but not in sufficient amounts to deliver independence – indeed Pamela explicitly warns against giving relatives more than they deserve, and no one except the heroine and her humble but worthy parents changes class. Money is properly used to relieve suffering or pay debts, not to reform hierarchy. The masters alone have superfluity; the others have just enough for gratitude but not enough for idleness. Only Mr Longman, the steward, amasses any fortune and he fittingly leaves it to the master from whom it was gained.

In *Grandison*, Sir Charles gives high value to fraternal and filial relationships which in turn make valuable all those ties that shadow them. To his extravagant, selfish and weak father, he responds with extreme filial piety, a piety born of Humean pride as much as Christian humility, so that in his eyes the paternal faults become manliness, nobility and 'magnificent spirit'. Sir Charles reverences all those of the older generation who are related to him and it is no wonder that the highest compliment to another is a statement of relationship – father or sister. Harriet Byron has a passion for transforming lovers into blood relatives and many of the most tearful scenes describe these sentimental transformations. As one would expect, the love and reverence that inform these equal familial ties and transformations are also displayed in the ties of servitude. Sir Charles, who requires kindness and compassion among his servants, automatically commands duty and loyalty:

> it was delightful to see the attention paid to him by the servants as they waited at table. They watched every look of his. I never saw love and reverence so agreeably mingled in servants' faces in my life. And his commands were delivered to them with so much gentleness of voice and aspect, that one could not but conclude in favour of both, that they were the best of Servants to the best of Masters. (I, p. 229)

In *Pamela* and *Grandison* ideal fellowship is domestic. For Harriet, quoting her grandfather, families are 'little communities' which help to secure 'the great community of which they are so many miniatures'. True to sentimental philosophy, the 'great community' is not the impersonal economic and political unit of the state but simply the sum of good Humean fellowship. Pamela's household is the microcosm of the great community; it is providential and the image used for it, of the 'clockwork' machine, is similar to that used by Newtonian poets for God's creation and dispensation.

The most potent force for community is emotional ritual or the display of sensibility, where the tearful master or mistress may show inferior spectators a posture of sympathy or a gesture that provokes responsive tears. In *Pamela* and *Grandison* a sense of community is constructed out of the immense reverence of social or moral inferiors for exemplary characters and their displays of heart. In the *Letter to d'Alembert* (1758) Rousseau had advocated emotional public rituals, unsophisticated festivals which would serve to unite the participants. He stressed the importance of the spectacle of these rituals in which many could participate, so learning and enacting unity. In *Pamela* such rituals function as small dramas or community services ending in outpourings by all the watchers, who are momentarily made equal in their tearful and choked response. Yet in reality hierarchy is, in Richardson's world, confirmed, not endangered, by these displays. As Pamela points out, a lady may in ritual emotional moments descend to her servants, while she can 'secure and even augment the respect and veneration of inferiors at the same time' (II, p. 145). Rituals and tableaux of community reach their apogee in the second part of *Pamela* where they are created and recreated in variation of the single scene until her brother-in-law gasps, 'There is hardly any bearing these moving scenes, following one another so quick.'

The most heady images of fellowship are constructed by women who recognize and accept male dominance but who may more easily display the sensibility that binds people together. Mr B provides the money but Pamela makes the fellowship. In *Grandison*, whose wandering hero is far from dominating the book, the blissful sentimental fellowship is most nearly approached in the parlour of Harriet Byron and her devoted friends and relatives and in the remembered domestic world of Sir Charles's excellent mother: 'Who will say, that mothers may not be the *most* useful persons in the family . . . Sir Thomas Grandison's delights centred in himself, Lady Grandison's in her husband and children. What a superiority, what an inferiority!' Her 'useful, prudent, serene, benevolent' life makes fellowship in the absence of the egocentric man (I, pp. 312–13).

Clarissa, where the men will not go away or serve the female communal aim, profoundly disturbs the construction of the familial fellowship of *Pamela* and *Grandison* since it allows aggressive men and masculine women to turn a family into a group of warring individuals. Civil war irrupts and all the mechanism of household is in disarray. Power uncoated with sentiment simply becomes patriarchal and repressive, and the women of the family display their tears in vain against 'the father's will'. Rousseauist rituals are denied and Clarissa, the most potent displayer of sentiment, is made impotent by imprisonment and isolation. Here, then, the image of sentimental fellowship is reduced and distorted until it can no longer express itself in the overflowing relationships of parent and child, brother and sister.

In *Clarissa* the familial fellowship of sympathy and benevolence dwindles and its place is taken only by the friendship of Clarissa and Anna Howe, two powerless women. The friendship works against, not with, society and is defensive, not expansive; yet it still remains the prime expression in the book of sentimental community and the familial tie.

Already in *Pamela*, friendship between tender, sympathetic women was described in terms of sensibility, thinning 'the animal man', running through the heart in a 'lify current', and providing a pale foretaste of a perfectly sympathetic heaven. In *Grandison*, strengthened by 'the mutual unbosoming of secrets', it combats depression and isolation: 'what a solitariness, what a gloom, what a darkness, must possess that mind that can trust no friend with its inmost thoughts!' (II. p. 165). But in *Pamela* and *Grandison* there is no pressing need of the defensive huddle of female friendship, which comes to the fore in *Clarissa*. In this novel, despite the heroine's manifest fears that close female friendship will have political and social implications, she and Anna Howe forge a bond which vibrates with all the sentiment of family and sympathetic fellowship and in its most ecstatic moments threatens to assume the role of romantic love:

> How much more binding and tender are the ties of pure friendship and the union of like minds, than the ties of nature!

Well might the sweet singer of Israel, when he was carrying to the utmost extent the praises of the friendship between him and his beloved friend, say, that the Love of Jonathan to him was wonderful; that it surpassed the *love of women*! What an exalted idea does it give of the soul of Jonathan, sweetly attempered for the sacred band, if we suppose it but equal to that of my Anna Howe for her fallen Clarissa! (III, p. 517).

Anna urges Clarissa against the 'old patriarchal scheme' into a sentimental retreat, where she would take her legacy and dispense charity, but Clarissa, too firmly trapped in the ideology of the family and of sentiment that exalts filial piety and domestic duty, and insists on women's subordination, cannot agree. Yet Anna remains for her the main earthly comfort, presenting the only relationship that opposes the acquisitiveness and cruelty of the non-sentimental male world.

In eighteenth-century poetry, there is a vacillation between joy in fellowship and desire for isolation. In *Clarissa* a yearning for solitariness is suggested but, since women are defined in relation to marriage, it expresses itself in a desire for the single state. Even before she is beset by Lovelace and other unsuitable suitors, she craves a retreat to her grandfather's house, although she also desires to be socially useful. But, as her family makes clear, such a craving is impermissible in a woman for whom there is simply no place of sentimental autonomy outside the 'little community' of the family. The only singleness she can achieve is in death and the only house she can inhabit alone is her elaborate coffin.

Language and letters

In the Preface to *Grandison*, Richardson describes his characteristic epistolary style as writing 'to the *Moment*, while the Heart is agitated by Hopes and Fears'. In concentrated form this is a typographically excited mode using a plethora of emphatic and repetitive devices and breaking the logical narrative surface with exclamatory irruptions. Used in a diluted manner by many correspondents to give dramatic excitement to their accounts, in its concentrated form it is most employed by Lovelace, who glories in his peculiar '*lively present tense* manner' and who eulogizes the familiar letter as 'from the heart (without the fetters prescribed by method or study), as the very word *correspondence* implied' (II, p. 431).

The connection with Lovelace suggests that this style, in its extreme form, can be associated with men's power of free social expression and with ebullient sexuality. It therefore becomes a difficult style for women, unless they declare their faults of insubordination like Anna Howe and Charlotte Grandison, and for exemplary male characters who deny sexual expression and conceal their social power. Clarissa, Pamela, Harriet and Sir Charles on the whole write carefully and precisely and their narratives are usually consecutive and logical. Even the mad Clementina, when she writes, manages to express herself with propriety and coherence. If women use the Lovelace kind of expressive language in concentrated form, they usually do so *in extremis*, when they are physically molested, frightened or agitated. In these cases, the style expresses sexual horror and social impotence rather than ebullience and freedom.

Because of their greater physical susceptibility and because of the social constraints on their verbal expressiveness, women are more sincere in gesture than in words in a social situation, and language frequently exists only to censor a truth expressed by the body. Over and over again in Richardson men speak messages but women convey them with a look. This relative lack of sincere female speech would seem to complicate Richardson's predication of the largest part of his novels on women's words – words which describe how their users were made speechless, passive and incoherent, or driven to silent fainting fits. A partial solution to the problem is emphasis on the letter form itself, which although apparently a distancing device – letters must follow events and express some detachment – in fact makes it possible for verbal expressiveness and sensibility to unite, without any touch of sexuality or impropriety.

From Richardson's outburst against spurious continuations of his novel, it seems that a letter could be ravished and sullied. The letter becomes an analogue to the sensitive female body, showing fragmentation and instability under stress and allowing violation. Often the analogy is openly declared in the novels and an invasion of private letters becomes an invasion of physical privacy, as when Mr B gropes about Pamela's person to come at the writings he wishes to read.

Like the body and unlike social speech, letters have some sincerity and spontaneity, both for the novelist and for his fictional characters. Although Richardson believed that an author should have a plan and fixed length in mind, he declared that he was not regular enough to compose in this way and that he hardly knew what he would write from one letter to the next. For the fictional characters, letters are a heart-expressing medium between organized prose and gesture, differing markedly from social speech: 'All of the Letters are written while the hearts of the writers must be supposed to be wholly engaged in their subjects,' Richardson wrote in the Preface to *Clarissa* (Penguin edn, p. 35). The reflection usually implied by words that are spoken in a social situation – reflection especially demanded of women – is avoided and the result is immediately affective.

In Richardson's rapturous assessment of the power of letters to communicate he is distinguished sharply from Dr Johnson, whose sense of the artificiality of any writing was acute. Richardson rejects the absolute insistence on artificiality, although he dramatizes the self-presentation of his correspondents, as well as the duplicitous evasions which Johnson considered always present in the act of writing. With all his knowledge of the fragility and vulnerability of letters, Richardson yet seemed to feel in some inexplicable way that they could, if honestly indited, bypass social speech and record the 'heart' of the writer.

The Richardsonian letter has some of the sincerity of the body then; it may reveal hidden traits, since it is created when the heart is engaged, even if it is ostensibly written after events. So it is possible to read letters like faces for both 'are indicative, generally beyond the power of disguise, of the mind of the writer'! But the letter form has a great advantage over the body as a way of expressing sensibility since it requires no present spectator. So, despite the analogies between physical gesture and letter that foster spontaneity, the letter form mitigates the seductive, 'inflaming' quality of physical sensibility which Richardson was so much at pains to quench; it therefore becomes a suitable sentimental expression for exemplary men and women who may write precisely, and also display some of the exuberance of style Lovelace took to an extreme.

At the same time the letter can allow communication without denying the withdrawal from society for which sensibility so often seemed to yearn. Sentimental letters, written in the isolation of the closet, can forge rapturous ties of fellowship, making 'distance, presence' and communicating feelings without intruding the difficulties of physical social presence. As Richardson expressed it in his correspondence: 'The pen is jealous of company' (*Selected Letters*, p. 66).

VI Fiction: The Man of Feeling

The bookseller in Thomas Bridges' *The Adventures of a Bank-Note* (1770–1) remarks that 'a crying volume . . . brings me more money in six months than a heavy merry thing will do in six years' (III, 5). The age wanted tales of misery and misfortune and it required a man of feeling to enter them. *Clarissa*'s overwhelming example set and dominated the pattern for the woman of sensibility, but the model of the socially potent and fulsomely admired Sir Charles Grandison with his Humean pride did not comprehend the lachrymose desires of the public for a man of sensibility who, continually suffering, would allow the luxury of sympathetic grief. This, by the mid–eighteenth century, had become one of the main pleasures of reading.

A spate of novels ministered to the taste, a few of which are still read: Sarah Fielding's *Adventures of David Simple* (1744 and 1753), Henry Brooke's *Fool of Quality* (1764–7), Oliver Goldsmith's *Vicar of Wakefield* (1766), Laurence Sterne's *A Sentimental Journey* (1768), in part his *Tristram Shandy* (1759–67) and Henry Mackenzie's *The Man of Feeling* (1771). They differ considerably in their presentation of male suffering and sensibility, but each grapples with the philosophical and narrative problems of what to do with the man of feeling who has, in an unfeeling world, avoided manly power and assumed the womanly qualities of tenderness and susceptibility but who cannot be raped and abandoned.

David Simple, *The Man of Feeling* and *A Sentimental Journey* can exemplify the point. Despite the unusual fact that it was written by a woman, *David Simple* typifies the serious plot of male sentiment and, with *The Man of Feeling*, it follows through its psychological and social logic; although the two novels are separated by almost two decades, together they catch the main myth of the literary cult of sensibility. Sterne's *A Sentimental Journey*, the only one of the three books that still holds a wide readership, tempers sentiment with self-mockery and humour, and presents the sensitive man as feeling heart, fallible human being and resilient *picaro*, moving on unmarred by the tears of the world. The last two authors, Mackenzie and Sterne, are, according to Sir Walter Scott, accepted as 'the most celebrated' of writers 'who are termed sentimental'.[1]

The plots

The action of *David Simple*, Part I (1744) tells of the sentimental search for a friend, 'a little Community as it were of two, to the Happiness of which all the Action of both should tend with an absolute disregard of any selfish and separate Interest'. By the end of Part I, miraculously, David has found more than one friend and has formed a fellowship of four victimized souls with whom to travel into the miseries of Part II.[2]

This part was added in 1753 after Sarah Fielding's vision had darkened and after the publication of *Clarissa*. In Part I David ends believing that tenderness can prevail in a very small secluded community which avoids the world. In Part II, as his little family is impoverished and depleted, he learns that benevolence and tenderness are not enough, for everyone is ultimately dependent on the vicious.

Sterne's *A Sentimental Journey* has no plot beyond a journey of the heart across the simplified social map usually followed by the wandering man of feeling. Yorick travels to France where he places or finds himself in various positions in which he can witness the spectacle of human emotions, from the melancholy madness of Maria to the poor man's grief for his dead ass. He acts and reacts spontaneously and emotionally, and describes his sensations; he exults in the sexual aspect of sensibility which, however, becomes not a threatening passion but a harmless and impotent enjoyment. Some readers, especially in the following century, considered *A Sentimental Journey* bawdy, but Sterne himself used the adjectives 'frolicksome' and 'chaste'. Indeed, with its whimsy and self-conscious coyness, the book gives the impression less of erotic struggle than of an old man's contentment at transitory human weakness and acceptance of only partial power and sensation (Sterne was ill when he wrote it and died shortly afterwards). The death which Yorick seems to be fleeing is not primarily the entry into an afterlife, however, or even a validation of emotion in this life, but simply a cessation of delicious human sensations. Yorick is a connoisseur of feeling rather than a man of feeling.[3]

The real man of feeling exists in one of the great blockbusters of sentiment, Mackenzie's *Man of Feeling*. The heir of *David Simple*, it has less intricacy of plot and much less acute psychological generalization than its forerunner. But the books come together in abandoning a compassionate, sensitive Shaftesburian soul in a materialistic, callous and Hobbesian world; although giving him ample justification for misanthropy or complete withdrawal, they allow him to arrive at his end essentially unchanged.

Mackenzie's Harley, an orphan of an ancient but impoverished family, is persuaded to go to London to try to obtain the lease of some adjacent lands, which might help his fortunes. Unfitted for the task and incipiently in love with his prosperous neighbour's daughter, Miss Walton – a beautiful woman already interestingly fading at 24 – he travels to London, where he is taken in by the usual poseurs: a footman pretending to be a gentleman and a gambler masquerading as a benefactor. Nevertheless, he meets also with real worth in the repentant prostitute Miss Atkins, whom he helps. Returning unsuccessful in his suit, he encounters a decrepit soldier in whom he discovers a childhood mentor, Edwards. The old man's sorry tale of misfortune and sacrifice – he has insisted on going as a soldier in place of his married son – wrings copious tears from Harley. When they arrive at their home, all is changed and Edwards's son is dead, leaving two orphan children. After much kindness to the unfortunate trio, Harley catches a fever while nursing Edwards; together with his untold love for Miss Walton, this brings about a debility that results in a welcomed death.

Instruction

Most sentimental novels with heroes insist on their instructional nature. But this becomes problematic as the cult of sensibility grows more self-indulgent and sensational. In the early, entirely non-naturalistic part of *David Simple*, the sentiments or moral reflections are delivered to edify the reader in the manner of the tags of sentimental drama. A character will learn with the reader that 'those People know very little of real Misery . . . who can be very solicitous of what becomes of them' or that 'it requires a very good Understanding to bear great Indulgence, or great Prosperity, without behaving ill, and being ridiculous'. Incidents occur solely for the maxims they produce, and there is no interest in the personalities necessary to create such incidents. Precise response is taught to both character and reader, who find, for example, that, after an affecting episode when a destitute man is helped, there are two possible stances: an ordinary person, that is a middling materialist, might see how pleased such a man would be to receive clothes, but a sensitive reader would sympathize with the more poignant emotion available to a sick man who accepts sudden kindness. In other places a reader learns that feeling is sometimes decently inarticulate and that silence is the proper response to great grief.

Although avoiding generalized morality, later works keep up the insistence on instruction through sentiments. Sterne told a friend that *A Sentimental Journey* was designed 'to teach us to love the world and our fellow-creatures better than we do', while Richard Griffith described *Tristram Shandy* as a work 'whose principal end . . . was to inculcate that great *Magna Charta* of mankind, humanity and benevolence'. The Advertisement to Sterne's complete works in 1780 declared that the more they were read the more benevolence would be fostered in society, while Thomas Jefferson asserted that Sterne's writings were 'the best course of morality that ever was written'.[4] Walter Shandy thought that everything has wit and instruction in it 'if we can but find it out'.

Mackenzie wrote to his cousin that his aim in his novel was not narrative but instructional: 'I was somehow led to think of introducing a Man of Sensibility into different Scenes where his Feelings might be seen in their Effects, & his Sentiments occasionally delivered without the Stiffness of regular Deduction.' The book would be 'as different from the Entanglement of a Novel as can be'. According to Mackenzie, the aim of reading is to indulge feelings: so he cautions his cousin not to read the chapter on the distressed father 'till you have a mind to indulge those Feelings which it endeavours to produce'. The result will be the reader's pleasure, 'that Pleasure which is alwise experienc'd by him who unlocks the Springs of Tenderness & Simplicity'.[5]

In these later works of the 1760s and 1770s, sentiments are clearly outflowings of emotion, rather than emotion combined with moral reflections, and characters teach response more than virtuous action. The hero is not a pattern for life, although authors still make the ritual claim. Primrose in *The Vicar of Wakefield*, for example, is for many modern readers a case study of sickly sensibility; yet the Advertisement describes him as exemplary. Yorick, Harley and Werther present such extremes of sensibility that they must be regarded as untypical and not exemplary in the manner of Grandison, although there were people who assumed the whimsies of Yorick and who allegedly killed themselves after Werther.

That the feeling responses in the books are paramount and that the story must subserve them is clear from the narrative form. There are hiatuses, fragmentations and, especially, repetitions, not in order to state a moral truth or impress a psychological trait, but simply to highlight and intensify an emotional effect. The prostitute Miss Atkins in *The Man of Feeling* tells her story once, and her father tells it a second time from his point of view, making little difference to the story but wringing from it yet more emotional drops.

> As I approached our little dwelling my heart throbbed with the anticipation of joy and welcome, I imagined the cheering fire, the blissful contentment of a frugal meal, made luxurious by a daughter's smile, I painted to myself her surprise at the tidings of our new-acquired riches, our fond disputes about the disposal of them. (p. 48)

When he finds she has gone, 'the gay visions with which I had delighted myself, vanished in an instant. I was tortured with tracing back the same circle of doubt and disappointment.' The value and authenticity of feeling makes verbal as well as narrative repetition inevitable. In March 1771, in a letter to his cousin, Mackenzie justifies having quoted his own book to her: 'when the same sentiments arise, much the same words present themselves to express them.'

Stories are told to display extremes of feeling. Old Edwards, the most artful manipulator of emotion in *The Man of Feeling*, describes a blissful domestic moment on Christmas Eve before introducing the horror of his departure as an aged soldier:

> 'Twas on a Christmas eve, and the birth-day too of my son's little boy. The night was piercing cold, and it blew a storm, with showers of hail and snow. We made up a cheering fire in an inner room; I sat before it in my wicker-chair, blessing providence, that had still left a shelter for me and my children. My son's two little ones were holding their gambols around us; my heart warmed at the sight: I brought a bottle of my best ale, all our misfortunes were forgotten.
>
> It had long been our custom to play a game at blind man's buff on that night, and it was not omitted now; so to it we fell, I and my son, and his wife, the daughter of a neighbouring farmer, who happened to be with us at the time, the two children, and an old maid servant, who had lived with me from a child. The lot fell on my son to be blindfolded: we had continued some time at our game, when he groped his way into an outer room in pursuit of some of us, who, he imagined had taken shelter there; we kept snug in our places, and enjoyed his mistake. He had not been gone long there, when he was suddenly seized from behind; 'I shall have you now,' said he, and turned about. 'Shall you so, master?' answered the ruffian, who had laid hold of him; 'we shall make you play at another sort of game by and by.' (p. 63)

Harley responds as he ought with tears and complete imaginative identification with the grief; the sentimental reader should copy him.

Clearly, instruction aimed at active virtue in life, the implied purpose of Part I of *David Simple* and the stated aim of *Pamela*, is no longer the aim of sentimental fiction. It is not even an education in sympathy that is primarily provided but rather a course in the development of emotional response, whose beginning and end are literary. The reader learns how to respond to fictional or narrated misery and how to read the tale. The emotion in the passage of Edwards is contrived, fictive, in no way a pattern for life, and it feeds into, rather than out of, the book.

Sentiment and sensibility

The sentimental novel is often said to be the vehicle of a sentimental philosophy positing innate virtue or goodness in all humanity. Nothing could be further from the scene presented in the majority of the novels. A single vulnerable hero is opposed to the expanse of a hostile society, and, while the sentimental Humean virtues of benevolence and tenderness are indeed the basis of human worth and fellowship, these virtues on the whole occur defensively and impotently and their possession always creates the victim. Moral optimism may be asserted but the vicious context of virtue is most stressed.

In both parts of *David Simple*, tenderness is the summary of sentimental philosophy. Occasionally an unwary reader might be tempted to see irony at the expense of the tender and simple David (similar to the self-irony of Sterne's Yorick), but the temptation should be withstood, for all tenderness in so bleak a world is to be respected. In *A Treatise of Human Nature* David Hume declared: 'A propensity to the tender passions makes a man agreeable and useful in all parts of life, and gives a just direction to all his other qualities, which otherwise may become prejudicial to society' (pp. 603–4). David Simple seems almost without other qualities for he is one 'on whose Tenderness the least Appearance of Grief in others made an immediate Impression'.

Tenderness is tied to instinctive benevolence and is opposed to right conduct based on principle. The rational case for the latter is made by Mr Orgueil:

> I look upon Compassion, Sir, to be a very great Weakness . . . the real Love of *Rectitude* is the Motive of all my Actions. If I could be moved by Compassion in my Temper to relieve another, the *Merit* of it would be entirely lost, because it would be done chiefly to please myself. But when I do for any one, what they have a Right to demand from me, by the Laws of Society and right Reason, then it becomes *real Virtue*, and *sound Wisdom*. (*David Simple*, p. 71)

Acting rightly from principle denies tenderness and compassion and leads to complacency; as Part II of *David Simple* reveals, it turns easily into cruelty. In *Grandison*, compassion and principle were brought together in the hero who indeed gave alms prudently and tenderly, but for many readers he also seemed inevitably marked by complacency.

The reasoned opposition to benevolence in *David Simple* makes it a more defined but also a more vulnerable quality, since it seems to contrast not only with indifference but also with any scheme for systematic improvement. Belief in some form of general improvement is, however, implied in *The Fool of Quality*, where the sentimentalist, believing that benevolence will reveal innate virtue in the apparently wicked, becomes a peripatetic benefactor. More socially optimistic than *David Simple*, it was reissued by John Wesley as an illustration of Methodism or 'the religion of the heart'.

The tendency of *The Fool of Quality* is towards heavenly validation of earthly benevolence. In *The Man of Feeling* this divine validation is combined with the social pessimism of *David Simple*, so that there is no suggestion that Harley's benevolence could ever extensively move outwards. He has few heirs and each is solitary, while his progress through the world seems quixotic, a problem of his perception as much as a criticism of society. The tempering of benevolence occurs not through disastrous experience or through reasoned arguments but more through figures who shadow the hero: Ben Stilton, the example of a contemplative sentimentalist who achieves an effect mainly in death; old Edwards, an active sentimentalist who learns that the son he suffered to save lost everything and missed his father before dying; a beggar who manipulates listeners into fraudulent generosity with fabricated stories when his real tale of woe failed to interest; and finally the misanthropist, a former sentimentalist who abjured sentiment when he found his friend and lady false and now points to the egoism he finds inherent in sentimental benevolence:

Whence is the luxurious happiness they describe in their little family circle? Whence the pleasure which they feel, when they trim their evening fires, and listen to the howl of winter's wind? Whence but from the secret reflection of what houseless wretches feel from it? Or do you administer comfort in affliction – the motive is at hand; I have had it preached me in nineteen out of twenty of your consolatory discourses – the comparative littleness of our own misfortunes. (*The Man of Feeling*, p. 28)

It is close to the point made in *David Simple* – the selfishness or gratification of compassion and benevolence – but there is in *The Man of Feeling* no argument against it, simply flight.

Benevolence aims to create ties, as in Richardson's novels. In *David Simple*, the ideal sentimental fellowship, posited for a few pages, is located in the family or in a small group taking on familial roles, all in flight from the world. It is a combination of the defensive alliance of Clarissa and Anna Howe and the outgoing households of *Pamela* and *Grandison*. The community in *Tristram Shandy* is small and confined; the closest ties are between men and, as in *A Sentimental Journey*, the most sentimental one is the nostalgic feudal bond of loving master and faithful man. Here is Trim telling his employer the sad tale of his brother:

> He was an honest, lighthearted lad, an please your honour, as ever blood warm'd—
> —Then he resembled thee, Trim, said my uncle Toby, rapidly.
> The corporal blush'd down to his fingers ends – a tear of sentimental bashfulness – another of gratitude to my uncle Toby – and a tear of sorrow for his brother's misfortunes started into his eye and ran sweetly down his cheek together; my uncle Toby's kindled as one lamp does at another; and taking hold of the breast of Trim's coat . . . as if to ease his lame leg, but in reality to gratify a finer feeling – he stood silent for a minute and a half.[6]

The sentimental fellowship of two or more people finds sociability within itself but confronts a vicious world. It tends, then, to escape as far as possible from others and to locate itself in the country. David Simple retreats there at the end of Part I only to find that virtue cannot be isolated; Shandy Hall is in the heart of the country, and the 'feast of love' in *A Sentimental Journey* is in a peasant's house far from Paris. Harley speedily leaves sophisticated London for the simple world of rural England, where he can patronize honest souls and play with children. The few books that try to image a better society generally find it not in any political or economic progress but in a re-establishment of a kind of nostalgic feudalism, making ties out of patronage and loyalty rather than out of the economic needs of the emerging capitalist order. As in Richardson and in the moral philosophers, the unit is the family or cluster of families, not the economically riven and socially fissured nation. This is so even in *The Fool of Quality* which, unusually for fiction but commonly for drama, makes the benefactor a merchant who has gained his wealth through trade; he distributes it, however, in New Testament fashion and retreats from the city where it was acquired.

Mostly the fictional sentimentalist is ardently anti-capitalist, despising those who hoard and increase money and dispensing his own wealth liberally and with speed. The vicious Mr Orgueil in *David Simple* is a kind of capitalist in both emotional and economic ways, lending only when sure of a gratifying return for his money or kindness. David simply expends. Reason barters but sentiment is a surplus in the economy with no exchange value. It is therefore expensive, and poverty is bound to be its companion.

And it is appropriate that it should be. For although several novels end with providential legacies – the two remaining women in *David Simple* are patronized by a person who never appears and Primrose's good nature in *The Vicar of Wakefield* is suddenly rewarded with money – the real element and test of sentiment is in poverty, which becomes the proper situation for the man of feeling, just as sexual assault became the right test for the woman.

The sentimentalist does not enter the economic order he condemns. He refuses to work to better himself or society. If he suffers great adversity – some complicated social catastrophe from outside to do with the law or a friend's collapse – he retrenches or takes up non-capitalist work, tending perhaps to a small garden which is as likely to breed flowers as turnips. Ownership of property which validates the gentleman in more naturalistic fiction, while it eases life and allows increased benevolence, is acceptable only when in benevolent or domestic service, when it aims to 'comfort a Family'; property to aggrandize the self makes its owner, in Sarah Fielding's words, 'degenerate into Filth and Nastiness'. Support is not earned but accepted by the man of feeling. As in Richardson's novels, money rarely alters although it can restore status, and it rewards pathos and surrender rather than struggle. The Vicar of Wakefield receives largesse only when he has accepted his sorry situation.

The giving of money is especially moving when the power of giving is accompanied by some weakness in the giver. So Yorick who admits he gives from the stirrings of sexuality and from a surrender to the modes of the world or Harley who gives on irrational impulse is a more affecting object that the compassionate but strong and prudent Grandison. The benevolist in *The Vicar of*

Wakefield sees his generosity springing from a benevolence imaged by physical disease:

> Physicians tell us of a disorder in which the whole body is so exquisitely sensible, that the slightest touch gives pain: what some have thus suffered in their persons, this gentleman felt in his mind. The slightest distress . . . touched him to the quick, and his soul laboured under a sickly sensibility of the miseries of others.[7]

The benevolent man who dispenses charity is given no monetary reward although he is usually paying for and expecting to be rewarded by an emotional display. In Bedlam, Harley gives money for the mad woman because she alone has called forth his tears:

> The unfortunate young lady had till now seemed entranced in thought, with her eyes fixed on a little garnet ring she wore on her finger; she turned them now upon Harley. 'My Billy is no more!' said she; 'do you weep for my Billy? Blessings on your tears!' . . . Harley looked on his ring.—He put a couple of guineas into the man's hand: 'be kind to that unfortunate'—He burst into tears, and left them. (*The Man of Feeling*, pp. 22–3)

Because of the emphasis on the emotional display, there is no opportunity to question causes. Harley does not stop to investigate the patriarchal power and rights that have brought the young lady to this madness. Often indeed the misfortune that is relieved has so complex an origin that no one social ill can be blamed. This is especially the case with old Edwards, whose disasters result from a muddled web of human unkindness, economic changes and personal incompetence. His eviction is presented to heighten pathos not to provoke social questioning:

> Had you seen us, Mr Harley, when we were turned out of South-hill, I am sure you would have wept at the sight. You remember old Trusty, my stag house-dog; I shall never forget it while I live; the poor creature was blind with age, and could scarce crawl after us to the door; he went however as far as the gooseberry-bush; which you may remember stood on the left side of the yard; he was wont to bask in the sun there; when he had reached that spot, he stopped; we went on: I called to him; he wagged his tail, but did not stir: I called again; he lay down: I whistled, and cried Trusty; he gave a short howl, and died! (*The Man of Feeling*, p. 62)

So too the injustice of conscription is deflected by the sacrificial posture of the old man, so touching that even the press gang is moved. The wars he enters are presented merely as a context for a benevolent act of Edwards towards an Indian, whose role in the story is not to display the miseries of colonialist exploitation but simply to play the noble savage and indicate movingly that benevolence may be instinctive in one or two members of any race.

Misery is alleviated by sensibility and sympathy, not by political action. As in Richardson's novels, communities are joined by sentimental displays and wordless gestures rather than by understanding and corporate struggle. The Shandy men are separated by obsessive thinking and by complete misunderstandings, but united through shows of grief or affection that momentarily cut through their inwardness. The sad event of Billy's death in *Tristram Shandy* does not in itself unite the Shandy household but the servant Trim reduces the kitchen to tears by the gesture it inspires of dropping his hat to the ground in a physical imitation of death. In *A Sentimental Journey* Yorick's tears tie him to the mad Maria and to the monk at Calais, while his palpitations link him to the lady from Brussels.

As Belford tells Lovelace in *Clarissa*, 'tears . . . are no signs of an *unmanly*, but contrarily of a humane nature; they ease the overcharged heart, which would burst but for that kindly and natural relief' (IV, p. 145). In sentimental men tears are mainly a response to the victim. David Simple on the whole cries for others and is silenced or subdued by his own sufferings.

The man of feeling cries easily and other benevolent characters share his tears. As in Richardson, so in this fiction, the body, now of the weakened or ageing man, becomes a true communicator beyond rational speech. When Miss Atkins's father is about to express his relenting but has not yet spoken it, 'his lip quivered, his cheek grew pale, his eyes lost the lightning of their fury . . . . He laid his left hand on his heart, the sword dropped from his right, he burst into tears' (*The Man of Feeling*, p. 46). The masculine sign of honour is here displaced by the more feminine posture of grief.

In Sterne's *A Sentimental Journey*, the body is a constant communicator. Physical well-being affects benevolence and the body's moods become the mind's: 'There is no regular reasoning upon the ebbs and flows of our humours.' The spontaneous, changeable and abrupt behaviour of the sentimentalist is tied to the surge in the arteries and the dilating of vessels; physical sensations reveal one person to another more sincerely than words: 'The pulsations of the arteries along my fingers pressing across hers, told her what was passing within me.'

The male body's sensitivity and susceptibility give some coherence to the plot of *A Sentimental Journey* and even include the author: as Sterne wrote in November 1767, 'I have torn my whole frame into pieces by my feelings . . . . I have long been a sentimental being.' God himself seems to grow physical and palpitating as he becomes the 'great SENSORIUM of the world' vibrating to and informing all human emotion: 'I feel some generous joys and generous cares beyond myself; all comes from thee, great, great SENSORIUM of the world! which vibrates, if a hair of our heads but falls upon the ground, in the remotest desert of thy creation' (*A Sentimental Journey*, p. 125). As R. F. Brissenden has noted in *Virtue in Distress* (1974), the Newtonian sense of the omnipresent deity permeating all things parallels the way the sentient principle of humanity, sensibility, informs the bodies of individuals.

The male body can express sensibility like the female. In Tristram Shandy Sterne wrote, 'A man's body and his mind . . . are exactly like a jerkin, and a jerkin's lining; – rumple the one – you rumple the other' (p. 127). But there is less emphasis on the authenticity of his gestures and signs – 'our minds shine not through the body, but are wrapt up here in a dark covering of uncrystalized flesh and blood' (p. 60) – and there are clearly problems with the expression. The sensitive body in women is inevitably sexualized for onlookers; this is appropriate since, although Richardson severs sexuality and sensibility in women, the plot of female sensibility is openly sexual. But no such plot is available to the man of sensibility, who operates in a scheme similar to the woman's, in which male sexuality implies mastery and dominance. So, to retain the 'female' qualities, the plot of the man of feeling is strangely desexualized, although its language may render the pathos erotic.

In *David Simple* sexual passion destroys tenderness since it demands instead of gives, and it undermines the sentimental fellowship of friends by substituting jealousy for generosity; true sentimental ties form erotically tinged relatives, not outright lovers. In Sterne, sexuality is diffused into happy whimsy and familial sentiment. The Shandy men appear emasculated in one way or another: Tristram has his nose damaged and cannot finish his autobiography; Mr Shandy is interrupted in his infrequent sexual act and cannot rear a son as he wishes; and Uncle Toby has a wound in his groin and is in full flight from the Widow Wadman. In *A Sentimental Journey*, Yorick fails to pursue the lady from Brussels, and encounters with women end in silence, unless the lady is a thousand miles away on a boat for India. Despite familial erotic sentiment, Yorick will never have a wife. In *The Man of Feeling*, Harley will not approach or confront the declining Miss Walton and would literally rather die than risk a response from her. In any case her appeal has been in the mode of sentiment, not sensuality: 'a blush, a phrase of affability to an inferior, a tear at a moving tale'. Sexual impotence or refusal, stressed more as the century progresses, goes some way towards bringing the male to the social condition of the female and so investing him with female sentimental significance: 'I am as weak as a woman', says Yorick with pride.

The ending of the man of feeling

The conclusion of *A Sentimental Journey* is a series of extreme sentimental sensations. First is the encounter Yorick seeks with Maria, which 'melts' nature within him and plays on the string of her melancholy love. He projects a scene of real comfort for her but, like many another man of feeling, does not enact it. The encounter is followed by the passage concerning God as 'great SENSORIUM' who vibrates like the poetic Aeolian harp. He becomes the source, the 'fountain', of the feelings of all people and by implication justifies his creation's inactive sensationalism. Next, Yorick experiences the paternalistic peasant farm and the 'feast of love', concluded by a dance of praise. This is a festivity, a rite of family and community, made into '*Religion*', a grace which touches and includes Yorick. Finally he faces the indecorous dilemma of two women and himself in a single room. The incident allows reference to his cough, which, with its implication of illness, makes the delicacies and gestures of life touching and a little silly. It ensures that the end clasp of the servant will be 'frolicksome', erotic, and not lewd, a very faint expression of the great all-justifying 'sensorium'. There can be no conclusion to such a plethora of incidents, experiences and ambiguities, and the only summary must be what Yorick once feared but also came to celebrate, that his virtues, his feelings, his sentimental effusions are 'the sport of contingencies'.

The author of *Critical Remarks* on Richardson, descanting on the unrealistic nature of Sir Charles Grandison, notes the impossibility of goodness and universal benevolence continuing into the 'world':

> [While] a human creature, in a simple unimproved state, is naturally generous and benevolent . . . when he comes abroad into the world, and observes the universal depravity of morals, and the narrow selfishness that every where prevail . . . he is either contaminated by the example, or contracts a misanthropical disposition. (p. 19)

The sentimental writers ignore this realism, and create heroes that remain innocent and uncorrupted, although they may certainly grow more melancholy and eccentric. In *The Vicar of Wakefield*, Sir William Thornhill, 'a man of consummate benevolence', goes so far in loving 'all mankind' that in the end he falls victim to improvidence and sentimental melancholy but he is never corrupted.

The male sentimentalist who is not peripatetic and not allowed the route of contamination or misanthropy is, however, caught in the financial and social logic of spontaneous benevolence. On the whole he follows a depressing trajectory. When David Simple dies, only a mother and daughter remain; the rest of his family and friends are dead of sickness, misery or starvation. Harley leaves two solitary 'ghosts'. The separation of the man of feeling from society continues to the end of his life and there is no reintegration in death through his obtaining a higher meaning for the 'world' he leaves.

The unredemptive death is especially poignant in *David Simple* where, towards the close of his life, the hero is forced like a woman into the cruel stasis of family and dependent friends. There are no longer tearful and affectionate family reunions as in *Pamela, Grandison* and *David Simple*, Part I, but only partings in death. The benevolent people become not redeemers but victims, prey to worldly predators. Clarissa died of the tensions of gender and sentiment in this world. Heaven in *David Simple*, captured, he had thought, on earth in the secluded community of Part I, is seen to be entirely distinct from it. The progress of the male sentimentalist in a depraved world is here towards crucifixion, but not a resplendent resurrection. All might be happy if all did their part, declares the narrator of Part I; in Part II selfishness conquers tenderness, and malice, envy, sickness, poverty and the law nullify benevolence. The family, so sanctified in Part I, now becomes a millstone round David's neck preventing him from insouciant benevolence and carefree escapism. The hero is 'entangled in the snare of his Love for others' and grows timid. Ultimately here sentiment bows before faith and resigns itself to Christian pessimism. David's review of his life is a philosophical summary of the problem of the incompatibility of sentiment and the world:

> Had anyone then attempted to persuade me, how little could I have believed, that the attaining a faithful and tender Friend, that strong Pursuit of my Life, and which I thought the Height of Happiness, should lead to its very contrary, and by that Means shew me the Short sightedness of all human Wisdom: Yet I found by Experience, that there are some Pleasures with which Friendship pays her Votaries, that nothing in this World can equal. But the same Experience has also convinced me, that when Fortune turns against us, she can point her Arrows with so much the sharpest Sting in her Quiver, that, when placed in the Ballance, more than weighs down all her highest Enjoyments . . . . I thought myself at home in this World, and attached my Heart to the Enjoyment of it, as strongly, though in a different Way, as does the Miser or Ambitious – . . . when Poverty broke in upon us, I found my Mind in such Chains as are much worse than any Slavery of the Body . . . my Eyes were forced wide open, to discover the Fallacy of fancying any real or lasting Happiness can arise from an Attachment to Objects subject to Infirmities, Diseases, and to certain Death; and I would not, for any Thing this World can give, lead over again the last Twelve-month of my Life. (pp. 430–1)

The harsh distinction of male sensibility from the world, the impotence that has no ultimate potency, is caught again in *The Man of Feeling*, which extends the ending of *David Simple* towards self-indulgence and greater escapism. David had at least entered the world of marriage and procreation, but Harley is essentially alone throughout his history. The problem of the sentimentalist's vulnerability in the world is not faced, as in the earlier novel, and the sweet melancholy of the hero's inevitable defeat and death covers the whole of his progress. Harley welcomes a death still young, for to avoid the misanthropic route he must die: 'I was not formed for the bustle of the busy, nor the dissipations of the gay.' The world for him has been 'a scene of dissimulation, of restraint, of disappointment' and he looks forward with some complacency to the 'genuine happiness' his virtue must have earned him.

Heaven alone might give meaning to Harley's route, although it is not a meaning to be appreciated in society, and he has long been living by its rules: 'The world is in general selfish, interested, and unthinking, and throws the imputation of romance or melancholy on every temper more susceptible than its own.' Adam Smith summed up his predicament:

> there is a helplessness in the character of extreme humanity which more than any thing interests our pity. There is nothing in itself which renders it either ungraceful or disagreeable. We only regret that it is unfit for the world because the world is unworthy of it.[8]

The logic of male benevolence is a death that has little of the power of Clarissa's, for sensibility is not primarily inherent in his body, although it palpitates, or in his gender. The Richardsonian woman's predicament is in the world; the man's is that he was essentially out of it. In fact he seems something of an exile from another realm, and his code of sensibility seems the rules of a non-earthly existence. His death appears inevitable and unshocking, for he is returning home without a struggle. In *The Sorrows of Young Werther* Goethe takes this process to its conclusion by allowing the sentimentalist to commit suicide. For Werther, innocence, sensibility and misery are so intertwined that God seems to have withdrawn from the earth.

Techniques

The sentimental text is necessarily fragmented – like sensibility that is inevitably expressed in moments. In Richardson's · novels fragmentation is expressed through the exigencies of the epistolary mode, for letters are physical objects that can be subverted, mutilated or lost. In *The Man of Feeling* the convention of editor and narrator allows interruptions, elisions and hiatuses. Parts of the narrative are declared to be lost – the beginning for example has been used for wadding a gun and other parts are suppressed or tampered with. The editor uses German philosophy for his wadding and Harley's aunt reduces another learned tome to a weight for pressing folds into linen; Harley himself leaves his love poem wrapped round the handle of a tea kettle. By these devices, stories, fictions or books are revealed to be not mind-possessing alternative worlds but simply vulnerable physical objects, fragments of experience to be buffeted about like the sensibility of the sentimentalist, 'the sport of contingencies'.

In *A Sentimental Journey*, the fragmentary nature of sentimental fiction becomes the organizing principle of the book. Each sentimental experience is momentary, a matter of heightened consciousness rather than event, and there can be no necessary ending. The story is a series of fragments, a progress through more and more places and more and more emotions. Its hero Yorick becomes a rake (but not of sexuality), a Casanova of sentiment, whose experiences do not impinge on the character and change it in any way. Sensibility does not inevitably learn or develop; if it does, it takes the trajectory of the Man of Feeling or Werther. Sterne's ending avoids this overt melancholy, but it is in its way sad, for the reader is suddenly and rudely returned to a world of time and consequence.

The first part of *David Simple* is episodic, openly didactic and closer in many ways to the exemplary narratives of sentiment or moral reflection in the *Tatler* and the *Spectator* than to Richardson's novels or to later, more naturalistic fiction. It pulls towards allegory and uncovers the general below the particular and the moral type below the accidents of manner and appearance. Beneath many characters are folk-tale stereotypes and fears: the witch stepmother, whose white skin would have grown 'black and hard' had it been properly 'an Emblem of her Mind', or the virtuous Cinderella orphan. In Part II of *David Simple* and in later sentimental novels, the characters remain stylized, with sensibility shown in conventional actions and in sentimental moments, not in development of personality. People are hobbyhorsical and mono-manic; they are blinkered by simple experience in their perceptions and caught in fixed associations of ideas, such as Locke likened to madness. Sterne's Uncle Toby finds battles everywhere; David Simple believes misfortune implies an unnatural brother such as he had once found. Each person encountered has a story, and his face is the book cover that may but should not belie the contents. Only the heroes have any detail lavished on them, and their fantasies and mental projections have the same status in the work as the characters they are described as meeting.

Women need to be kept to episodes but within these they may enter the patterns of the feminocentric novels. For example Cynthia in *David Simple* is involved in a family conflict which she wins not through triumphing in a struggle but through duty and passivity; her reward is the symbolic emasculation of the patriarch, his transformation into a weeping man of feeling. A similar scene occurs in *The Man of Feeling*, where Miss Atkins, whose seduction and abandonment lead to no questioning of the social order or the double moral standard, takes on the posture of the suffering Magdalen with the conventional and effective detail of her hair strewn about her shoulders. The picture so prevails on her incensed father that he dissolves into tears.

Mad women are especially suited to the episode. Their madness is usually not the disturbing and temporary one of an eminently sane woman like Clarissa, but rather a permanent and unquestioned madness usually dependent on the absolute loss of a man and forming the sufferer into a perpetual victim. Ophelia with her tuneful and flowery lunacy is the prototype of Sterne's melodious Maria with her loose hair and trickling tears and of the fair singing inmate of Bedlam in *The Man of Feeling*. In each of the novels female distress enhances the story and reveals the man of feeling, but is not allowed to dominate. In *The Vicar of Wakefield* authorial irony diffuses the female plot of seduction that could have been exploited; it becomes dominant, however, in a Victorian stage melodrama of the book written in 1878 by W. G. Wills entitled *Olivia*.

In *The Man of Feeling*, the allegorical method of *David Simple* is replaced by a method of abstraction and personification. Mental operations are not psychological processes but psychodramas. A soldier's honour wars with his heart and Harley in his benevolence is divided between qualities:

> Virtue bade him consider on whom he was going to bestow it [his shilling]. Virtue held back his arm; but a milder form, a younger sister of Virtue's, not so severe as Virtue, nor so serious as Pity, smiled upon him; his fingers lost their compression, nor did Virtue offer to catch the money as it fell. (p. 14)

In *A Sentimental Journey* the mind becomes a theatre in which unexpected actions are played and replayed. When Yorick ungraciously refuses alms to the monk in Calais, his heart upbraids him and his imagination replays the scene adding new lines. Thought and self-analysis are dramatized and externalized. Psychological processes are expressed further in physical sensations; writing itself causes a standing coach to move as if travelling on an imaginary journey, and the agitation of the coach is contemplated by spectators responding as if they were present at a theatrical show.

A man of 'female' feeling may embarrass the reader and various devices of narration seem designed to relieve this possible response. Consequently, the sentimental hero rarely has the affective impact of Richardson's heroines. In *Tristram Shandy*, the narrative stance of Tristram allows the reader to feel with the tearful Toby and Trim but also to be conscious of this sympathetic feeling and, sometimes, to be aware of his or her own superiority to the characters' unawareness. Tristram as narrator encourages the reader to smile benignly at his own whimsies, his black page denoting mourning and death, or his long-winded descriptions that puncture the mood of sentiment at its moment of creation. In *A Sentimental Journey*, where the sentimentalist is the narrator, the first person method prevents the depiction of a totally instinctive *ingénu* like Harley or the David Simple of Part I.

In *The Man of Feeling* there is an effort at distancing through the elaborate layering of narration. There are at least four interferences with the text before we have it (narrator, editor, clergyman owner and another person suggested by the editor when he asserts that the few political remarks are in a strange hand). On the extreme edge, the sporting curate shows the world's indifference to the man of sensibility when he uses the story of griefs and tears to wad his gun, so marring the tale as the world mars the life of the sensitive man.

Yet, despite this device, *The Man of Feeling* lacks much distancing, primarily because the narrator, who should provide it, clearly fails to do so. Hence perhaps its speedy susceptibility to changing taste which *The Vicar of Wakefield* and *A Sentimental Journey* have survived. In the beginning of the novel, the narrator, named Charles only on the last page, reveals a slight satiric bent; he has the detachment to set up two value systems, the worldly and the sentimental, and to observe that for happiness the sentimentalist must be unpolitical or else he will forever be 'quarrelling with the disposal of things'. He can also slightly mock Harley in his dealings with women, noting especially the naïveté of his responses and his

uselessness when a lady faints. This mockery fits ill with the image
of him which the editor created – of a 'grave oddish man' called
'The Ghost' who enjoys the company of children.

In the end the events described in the tale presumably defeat his
irony, and his slight mockery wilts under the onslaught of the
consummate manipulator of sentiment, Old Edwards. When
Harley is caught in the trivial but resonant act of forming a toy mill
for Edwards's grandson, Charles is moved to utter: 'it was a scene
of tranquil virtue to have stopped an angel in his errands of mercy!'
By the closing pages he is the complete sentimentalist, companion
and heir of Harley, sitting with him in the graveyard and insanely
interpreting a world of sentimental signs.

The novels of the sentimental man are offsprings of *Don Quixote*,
with its portrait of the idealistic *ingénu*. With the Spanish knight,
the man of sensibility goes through the world like a naïve child,
whatever his age. To some extent he is the equivalent both of the
Rousseauist noble savage, untamed by the corruptions of society
and trivial education, and of the wandering stranger of satire who
turns his simplifying gaze on the foolishness of men.[9] He resembles
too the madman whom Michel Foucault discovered inhabiting the
classical age of the eighteenth century in *The Order of Things* (1966,
trans. 1970); in a time of calculation, discernment and distinction,
he is an accepted deviant, marginal and different because unaware
of differences, expecting meaning simply to inhere in appearance –
as Harley and Charles do at the end of *The Man of Feeling* – and
require no intellectual decyphering.

With his expressed opposition to the mercantile ethos of the age,
the man of feeling seems to have delighted those who would have
had no part of his habits in life; ultimately he was unthreatening and
required no deep engagement or ideological involvement. Yet the
public did wish to see an image of him in life and they pushed an
identification of author and creation. This would have been entirely
inappropriate for a woman, whose sensibility is most displayed in
seduction and rape, or for Samuel Richardson, who associated
some of his friends with lesser characters but never himself with his
exemplary female heroes or heroines (or indeed with his gay
seducers) – 'I am not solicitous to establish a private Reputation for
Tenderness of heart', he wrote in a letter. To some extent
Mackenzie, a shrewd Scottish lawyer, fostered the identification
when he quoted himself and aligned his own feelings with those of

his creation. More thoroughly Sterne encouraged his own cult, publishing his actual sermons as *The Sermons of Mr Yorick* and making both himself and Yorick sentimentally in love with the Eliza who punctuates *A Sentimental Journey*.

Yet in spite of the accepted nature of his deviance and the desire to discover him in life, and in spite of the fact that contemporaries on the whole seem to have read the novels as they were supposed to read Richardson – for the sentiment – whether emotional display or moral reflection, the man of feeling remains an awkward figure with his chosen female helplessness. Consequently this fiction frequently holds the possibility of ironic reading beyond the prompted mockery of the narrators and their detached stance. So later ages in particular regarded these novels of sensibility wryly and have speculated that *A Sentimental Journey* is not simply a humorous and self-consciously sentimental work but entirely a satire on sentiment and that *The Vicar of Wakefield* is through and through a creation of irony.[10] Such a reading would be quite impossible in the epistolary novels of female sensibility and inappropriate to their grim or fantastic plots.

VII *Fiction: The Woman of Feeling*

'I know not if there is really a sex in the soul', mused a character in Henry Mackenzie's novel *Julia de Roubigné* (1777), 'custom and education have established one, in our idea . . . . There is a little world of sentiment made for women to move in, where they certainly excel our sex.'[1] In a letter of 1751, Richardson wrote that he favoured the image of the good woman over that of the good man, since 'Softness of heart, gentleness of manner, tears, beauty will allow of pathetic scenes in the story of the one, which cannot have a place in that of the other' (*Selected Letters*, p. 180). The cult of sensibility stressed those qualities considered feminine in the sexual psychology of the time: intuitive sympathy, susceptibility, emotionalism and passivity.

Women's unique sexual suffering, along with their bodily authenticity – their ready use of tears, blushes, palpitations, hysteria and even death – meant that they could, without incurring the charge of insufferable Grandisonian complacency, glorify themselves and be glorified in fiction. As May Sinclair remarked in 1912 of the biological 'one-sided arrangement', the fact that 'only one sex should pay in Nature' economy' meant that inevitably there was 'a profounder feeling, a finer moral splendour, a superior sex virtue in the sex that pays'.[2]

Depictions of women's 'moral splendour', idealizations of 'the sex that pays', are scattered over eighteenth-century fiction and conveyed in plots and characters of considerable stylization. These plots might roughly be divided into four types: those conveying, first, the faithful wife; second, the mother; third, the benevolent and sensitive virgin; and, fourth, especially after Rousseau's *La Nouvelle Héloïse* in 1761, the chaste, susceptible and unwilling wife.

Plots

Male creators of female exemplars much appreciated the faithful wife. In 1714 the *Spectator* announced of a woman: 'All she has to do in this world, is contained within the Duties of a Daughter, a Sister, a Wife, and a Mother.' It considered that 'a right Woman . . . should have a gentle Softness, tender Fear, and all those parts of Life, which distinguish her from the other Sex; with some Subordination to it, but such an Inferiority that makes her more lovely' and it gives these words to the wifely paragon: 'I . . . have no other Concern but to please the Man I love: he is the End of every Care I have.'

Rousseau's Sophie in *Emile*, the ideal education of a man, was a being raised to attain such subordinate perfection. Richardson's Pamela, 'an affectionate *wife*, a faithful *friend*, a polite and kind *neighbour*, an indulgent *mother*, and a beneficent *mistress*', as her author expresses it, is the great fictional model; despite her sprightliness in Part I, she learns obedience in all areas in Part II, even when wifely duty conflicts with judgement. Another is Henry Fielding's eponymous heroine, the loving and forgiving Amelia, married to a generous rake, that favoured character of male novelists and dramatists.

Women writers usually paid lip-service to this extraordinary wifely ideal. But, after the mid-century, they tended to change the emphasis, so that the contingency of the long-suffering wife was obscured by her worldly as well as spiritual potency. In Sophia Lee's 'The Two Emilys' of *The Canterbury Tales* (1798), the heroine has such exquisite and palpitating sensibility that a cross or crass word from a man well nigh annihilates her; her qualities of utter submissiveness, passivity and sweetness are rewarded in this world not only as in *Pamela* and *Amelia* by the affection of the husband, but also by power over him despite her rhetoric of submission.

On the whole, however, the harsh reality of eighteenth-century marriage enshrining absolute male power probably urged women writers in particular to turn from eulogies of wifeliness towards the glorification of the mother, to whom they gave a wonderful potency, especially over men. Other facts were no doubt also in play, possibly the changing status of motherhood, becoming a profession for women excluded from or disinclined to enter the market-place and denied any economic function in the home. Another factor might have been the large number of women authors writing from failed marriages that had left them with an ideology of submission and a reality of, in Charlotte Smith's case, an absent spouse and nine dependent children. Other women writers, painfully avoiding marriage, may have had difficulty envisaging a happy and legally acceptable union. Mary Wollstonecraft, author of *A Vindication of the Rights of Woman* (1792), became an unmarried mother, and one of her friends, Mary Hays, suffered ridicule because of her expressed love for a man indifferent to her; another friend, the poet and chronicler Helen Maria Williams, was vilified for associating with a married man. All three were writers of sentimental novels.

In fictional terms the move to motherhood was a clever one since the mother, unlike the wife, could be exalted without the problem of her social and legal subordination. Jane West, a conservative novelist of the 1790s and early 1800s, makes the mother into a redemptive figure with social power through control over her children, but the tone of almost religious reverence is caught by the Gothic novelist Elizabeth Helme, whose *St Margaret's Cave* (1801) has the still unacknowledged mother provoke this response:

> The lady Adelaide is not formed to create loose desires. Had you seen her, you would have felt the truth of what I assert; for dark indeed must that heart be, that could regard her with less reverence than that with which she inspired me . . . . I regarded the lady Adelaide with an admiration as pure, as I should have felt for a celestial being, suddenly placed before me, and with equal reverence, I could have fallen at her feet.[3]

Although they could express the wish fulfilment of both men and women, neither wife nor mother had, in the heyday of the sentimental novel, the real resonance of female sensibility, which needs some action to display itself, some male aggression and sexual power to threaten it. Richardson's Clarissa is obviously the model and her well-known fate ensured that the sentimental virgin should die – virginity leading neither to marriage nor to death was rarely desirable. The man of feeling had died, but his death had not achieved the mythic grandeur of Clarissa's; he was leaving a realm in which he had little concern and into which he had in a way been exiled, while by his death his values became even more separate from the values demanded from living economic men. But the death of the sentimental heroine was the extension of those values preached for women and their ultimate validation.

Yet women writers appeared to be uneasy at this death, although several depicted it, including two sentimental writers of the 1760s, Charlotte Brooke and Frances Sheridan. They differed from Richardson, however, since misunderstanding rather than the whole logic of the socio-sexual situation led to the sentimental deaths they described. In Charlotte Brooke's *The History of Lady Julia Mandeville* (1763) the event brings not the religious experience of *Clarissa* but a contained blasphemous question from the sprightly lady (a conventional character, after Anna Howe), who asks of the unnecessary death whether one dare 'arraign the ways of Heaven'. More evidently it delivers a 'voluptuousness of sorrow' in the already virtuous, when agony gives way to 'that pleasing melancholy' which 'is one of the most charming sensations of the human breast'. The mythic element is not caught, and the reader is left merely with the depressing suspicion that the bad will always prosper. Frances Sheridan's *Memoirs of Miss Sidney Bidulph* (1761) responds to the Clarissa myth by exaggerating the heroine's miseries until they become almost insupportable. Indeed Dr Johnson wondered whether she had a moral right to make her readers suffer so much.

Other women writers wanted the social power that only Clarissa's death delivered to her in the world of male sexual economy, while avoiding the rape that precipitated this death. Some female readers of Richardson had similar desires. Lady Echlin, one of the group of female friends and correspondents who minutely discussed his novels, was profoundly shocked by the ultimate male assertion of the rape but identified with the Richardsonian image of powerful female virtue: 'I felt', she wrote, 'Emotions not to be describ'd; and was too much oppresst, or distracted, to admit a rational sensibility to take place.' So shocked was she that 'this accomplish'd Libertine [was] not reformed by Clarissa's virtuous conversation' that she composed an alternative rapeless ending in which Lovelace, innocent of the final outrage, 'renounc'd his former wicked attachment, became a sincere convert, spent the twelve months he survived Clarissa, in imitating his dear departed; constantly observing her pious way of life.'[4]

The final type of plot became popular after Rousseau published *La Nouvelle Héloïse*, in which he describes the sentimental and sexual love of the heroine, Julie, for her young tutor, Saint Preux. The love is opposed by her father, who persuades her to marry his friend, an older man of wisdom and benevolence, with whom in time she establishes a model community of dependants and relatives. But Julie remains torn between the two men and the routes through life that they offer, and her early, public death is welcomed as a release. English variations of this plot tended to move it towards the Richardsonian construction, avoiding the sexual slip and making the heroine as pure as Clarissa; meanwhile the husband became more threatening and the lover more chaste.

In the later eighteenth century, the plots of virgin and unhappy wife predominate and can best exemplify the woman of feeling. Female writers often tried to appropriate the powerful myth of redemptive, passive femininity of *Clarissa*, while allowing the fantasy of worldly power in *Pamela*. A host of women could exemplify, among them the professional writers who proliferated in the 1780s and 1790s when the sentimental style was firmly established and sensibility as extreme emotionalism and refinement was opening itself most completely to attack.

Charlotte Smith's *Emmeline* (1788) is an instance of the fantasy of the powerful virgin. In this novel an orphaned girl manages, without offending propriety, to resist and eventually overpower both an uncle-guardian who has taken her patrimony and his son who intemperately desires her, as well as keeping at bay a host of vulgar middle-class friends among whom she must live. As the cousin dies of his own ebullience and intemperance, she emerges wealthy, triumphant and married to the man of her choice, a modest but worthy second son.

The Rousseauist novel of family against love is typified by *Julia de Roubigné*, Mackenzie's depiction of the woman of feeling. In this work, the author has an easier narrative time than in his earlier *Man of Feeling* since the female love plot has so definite a shape that happy marriage or death is almost inevitable, and the protagonist need not slip from life like Harley.

In the novel a noble though rather irritable father is made poor through a lawsuit. He is helped by a new neighbour, the morose but worthy Montauban, with whom he grows intimate and who falls in love with his daughter, Julia. She, however, loves the young Savillon, who has gone to sea to mend his fortunes, without having first declared the love he feels for her. Mistakenly she learns that Savillon is married and, pressed by her debt-ridden father and dying mother, she submits to a wedding with Montauban, only to learn later that Savillon has returned unattached. Her acceptance of a single meeting of farewell with her beloved provokes Montauban to such jealousy that he poisons his wife; when, as she is dying, she tells him of her innocence, he is maddened and poisons himself. The protagonists are, the final writer asserts, to be pitied not blamed.

A problematic variation of this Rousseauist plot is Mary Wollstonecraft's *Mary, A Fiction* (1788), where the narrative of love, duty and reconciling death breaks down and where the fantasy of powerful passivity caught in *Emmeline* turns sour.[5] It is the story of a sensitive, unappreciated girl who is pressed into marriage for economic reasons by her family. Consummation is delayed because of the youth of the partners and in the meantime Mary seeks a sentimental relationship first with Ann and then with the invalid Henry, both of whom die leaving her to death or death-in-life with the unknown husband. The Advertisement of the novel boasts that its heroine is not a Richardsonian or a Rousseauist heroine but a unique 'thinking woman'.

The plot of most fiction with women protagonists tells of female innocence and passivity endangered by aggressive male libertinage or parental power. Novels of virtuous virgins and unhappy wives such as the three described above follow a pattern. After a blissful childhood, the typical heroine loses her mother or mother surrogate at puberty and discovers that her father or surrogate father has been transformed into or displaced by a desiring and threatening man. The alliance in *Clarissa* of the persecutor Lovelace and the Harlowe men, together with the sudden retreat of the once apparently approving Harlowe women, captures this transformation. The aim of the heroine is to own herself in some way, to marry if and whom she wishes, while keeping the Richardsonian filial piety intact.

In *Emmeline* the heroine is already orphaned, losing her substitute mother at 15 and struggling thereafter with the desire of her aggressively sexual cousin aided by her acquisitive uncle. The plot can be read as Emmeline's fight for exogamy, to escape the sexual and economic trammels of the family. In *Julia de Roubigné* the impoverished father is helped by Montauban who presses his suit on Julia as her suffering 'angel' mother dies. Montauban is an intimate of her father and his equivalent in touchiness, misanthropy and jealousy in honour. In *Mary, A Fiction* the heroine is forced into marriage by her father and makes her dash for freedom as her mother dies.

Once the marriage of Julia de Roubigné is brought about, the father droops and declines rather as Julie's father had done in *La Nouvelle Héloïse*. In many female novels, the patriarchal father is humbled before his death and he becomes simply an erring, imprisoned or wilting parent to whom the dutiful daughter of superior morality reverentially ministers, like Cordelia or like the poetic maidens of Helen Maria Williams. Julia exclaims of herself that 'she should have shared the prison of her father in the pride of adversity; behold her now the partner of his humiliation!' Plots often resolve themselves into tableaux of dying fathers dominated by loving, sensitive daughters, a motif much employed by Dickens. But these *pietàs* are not dynamic and there are few social implications from the reversal of power. The father can commit no further action except dying.

Characters

In *Sir Charles Grandison* there was much comment on the hero's assumption of the female virtues of modesty and chastity; Richardson described how Colley Cibber mocked him for his 'male-virgin'. In women's fiction the process of 'feminization' and desexualization of the men – as well as of the exemplary women – goes a stage further.

The hero of *Emmeline* is passive and gentle beside the passionate, mercurial and threateningly sexual cousin he replaces in the heroine's life and affections. The beloved in *Julia de Roubigné* is a man of feeling, 'gentle, modest, retired', a man who answers to her vision of a husband not of stern and manly firmness, but of 'yielding weakness'. Savillon has been loved from childhood as a brother, since he and Julia shared the same nurse, and their affection is tender and unmenacing: 'In truth my story is the story of sentiment.' Wollstonecraft's hero, who fills the role of the absent husband and the dead woman friend, is a melancholy invalid and lacks male sexual aggression. The relationship he offers is ideal-parental and dependent; he treats Mary as 'a darling child' and pleases her with his fatherliness, while he requires her physical maternal care. In Sophia Lee's 'The Two Emilys' in *The Canterbury Tales* the feminization is seen nakedly in terms of power. The hero learns to eschew the masculine public world and the values of effort, action and reason: as the author puts it, he does not diverge 'from the sphere of so dear an attraction'. Emily explicitly asserts female sentimental values over male ones and sees them triumphing in this world without the sacrificial death of Clarissa.

Besides the romantic plot with its fantasy of gentle men, sentimental novels tend to have a plot of female friendship, partly no doubt because of the demands of epistolary fiction and partly because of Richardson's influential picture in *Clarissa*. As constructed in women's fiction of the last half of the century, this friendship is deeply sentimental; the most emotional tableaux and postures emerge from reunions and separations of female friends, and familial fellowship is frequently reduced, as in *Clarissa*, simply to a couple of persecuted and defensive female friends clinging together against a hostile world. In its ending Charlotte Lennox's *Euphemia* (1790) looks forward not to happy marriage, for this has been made impossible for the much-tried heroine, but to the sweetness of women's society.

In *Julia de Roubigné* the two chief correspondents follow the Richardsonian model of one sentimental and one spirited friend. Julia and Maria are so close that writing between them is 'only another sort of thinking'. An expression of heart and sympathy, the friendship was formed 'in the blissful period of infancy' and is ratified by Maria's promise that misfortune will never destroy it. Julia's final dying memory is of her friend: 'I imagine I feel the arms of my Maria thrown round my neck – her tears fall on my bosom!' (p. 151).

Mary, A Fiction takes the convention to an extreme where it begins to disintegrate. Wollstonecraft wrote the novel in a mood of self-pity when she was a governess in Ireland, and it confusedly investigates her own relationship with Fanny Blood, a relationship that had dominated her early adulthood, and that, in its disappointments and divided loyalties, refused to conform to the image of confidential female friendship Wollstonecraft had derived from sentimental literature. Friendship in the book fails to be a refuge in a patriarchal world and instead becomes a troublesome adolescent tie, both expressing and frustrating desire. It is only when the friend enters the feminine sentimental scheme of dying victim and becomes a pure object of benevolence that the relationship settles into the conventional mould and Mary can wholeheartedly assume the sentimental posture.

Like the fiction depicting men of feeling, novels with women of sensibility encourage the social fantasy of loyal service. Servants of the noble protagonists are familial and feudal, tied to their masters and mistresses through sentiment, not money. In *Emmeline* the faithful servant distinguishes the aristocratic heroine from the bourgeois employer who cannot imagine bonds with no commercial purpose. In *Julia de Roubigné*, the impoverished family remains well served by domestics who sob at their masters' sufferings and refuse payment for their services. Le Blanc, the faithful retainer, gives this account of the family's efforts at dismissing him:

> He held out the gold to me: I drew back; for I would not have touched it for the world; but he insisted on my taking it, till I fell on my knees, and entreated him not to kill me by offering such a thing. At length he threw it down on his table, and I saw him wipe his eyes with his handkerchief.—My dear master! said I, and I believe I took hold of his hand, for seeing him so made me forget myself.—He waved his hand for me to leave the room; and, as I went down into the kitchen, if I had not burst into tears, I think I should have fainted away. (p. 49)

As Savillon says of Julia's father, he 'has not one relation who has stood by him in the shipwreck of his fortunes; but the storm could never sever from their master his faithful Le Blanc.' Julia's maid Lisette writes that she 'would do any thing to serve' her mistress.

As the wish-fulfilment of all ill-educated girls, the sentimental heroine is exemplary in accomplishments, rather like Fielding's Tom Jones, who finds time from whoring and hunting to excel in Latin grammar and formulate precisely proper views on the contemporary English stage. Julia de Roubigné wishes to talk of books rather than gossip, and knows of music and painting. Like many of her fictional sisters, Wollstonecraft's Mary is versed in introspective poetry and possesses a much used copy of Thomson's *Seasons*; Smith's Emmeline made herself mistress of every useful and ornamental feminine employment 'without any instruction'. Clearly the heroine must have all cultural advantages while not compromising, with formal education, her status as victim.

Beauty and breeding are equally necessary. The tie made by Shaftesbury of ethics and aesthetics in popular thought, together with the emphasis on communication through the female body, had almost ensured that female beauty would denote moral worth. But in the sentimental novel of women it argues birth as well. Pamela was uncomfortably truly a servant girl and not only Fielding found her status hard to swallow (in the many adaptations and simplifications of the story, one constant is the discovery of her higher birth). The sentimental heroine, like Mary in Wollstonecraft's novel, Emmeline and the many Julias, will usually be proved well-born.

But aristocracy in the female novel is not linked with social power and privilege. Instead it is a mingling of élitism, sensibility and impotence. Its purpose is to oppose insensitivity and power and to rebuke the middle class. (The taunting of the bourgeoisie, a cliché of the sentimental novel, may seem a remarkable sort of self-abuse since the readership was largely from this class, but in fact the criticism is only partial, not of money but of inhumane obsession with money.) If gender is translated into class terms, the confrontation of female impotence and male economic power becomes a less disturbing one for women: that between the economically powerful, insensitive middle class and an impotent but refined aristocracy. Rank in women is, then, an exaggeration of what were considered peculiarly female qualities, rather as, in contrary fashion, in men it underlines masculine qualities – Richardson's Lovelace is an example.

If the noble woman acquires money, it will not be through work, but effortlessly, like the Vicar of Wakefield. It will somehow be her right by virtue of her very being. And she will, with Emmeline and Wollstonecraft's Mary, use it in the manner of sensibility instead of commerce. She will not employ it to increase wealth, as the middle-class capitalist would, but simply spend it to gratify others. In *Mary, A Fiction* the heroine uses her money to support her woman friend and any unfortunates she can discover; at the end of *Emmeline* the heroine receives the hereditary riches and uses part of them to patronize her friend and rid her of her useless spouse. The tender hero of *Julia de Roubigné* says of 'power and wealth' that 'to possess them . . . is nothing', but to use them benevolently 'is rapture'.

Above all, the sentimental heroine is characterized by superlative sensibility, conveyed in a series of stylized actions and physical demonstrations. She has, in David Hume's phrase, a 'propensity to the tender passions' and she is alive to the nuances of feeling. Her stance, like that of the man of feeling and David Simple, is overtly exemplary in response. She cries at a play when the insensitive are tearless. All such heroines convey their virtue through their meaningful bodies, and the most authentic emotions are signalled not by words but by tears, blushes, palpitations and fainting fits. Julia is the epitome of 'feminine softness' and her eyes are animated by sensibility. Feelings are her conscience and her soul informs her body; her appearance affects spectators by giving them a 'throb of virtue'.

In her story Emmeline has the opportunity to display all the weapons of impotence, the physical symptoms of sensibility, through her susceptible body. These symptoms become, in a political sense, variations of the manipulation of death, so powerfully employed by Clarissa. But Emmeline avoids death; like Pamela, Harriet and Ann Radcliffe's Emily in the *The Mysteries of Udolpho* (1794), she faints to good effect and overcomes her abductor with a well-timed fever. The second heroine runs mad and faints almost to lifelessness, a necessary extremity since she was sexually guilty and must neurotically suffer a substitute death to cleanse her sin.

In *Mary, A Fiction*, Wollstonecraft also accepted the image of superior female sensibility, privileged even when it verges on the excessive and diseased. But it is not the noble and public excess of Clementina in *Sir Charles Grandison* which could be displayed to and tempered by onlookers, but something closer to the melancholia of the graveyard poets. So there is neither cure nor any obvious narrative for the heroine to enter: 'her sorrows were her own . . . the black wave rolled along in the same course: it was equal to her where she cast her eyes; all was impenetrable gloom' (p. 56).

The heroine of sensibility is consumed with benevolence. Emmeline does good instinctively and Julia, even in relative poverty, dispenses 'mirth and gaiety to some poor families' of the neighbourhood. Mary Wollstonecraft's Mary is equally benevolent and she rivets the hero to her with her philanthropic postures: 'I would give the world', he exclaims, 'for your picture, with the expression I have seen in your face, when you have been supporting your friend' (p. 48).

None the less there is in *Mary, A Fiction* a difficulty over the benevolent route for women. The heroine's progress seems the conventional one of philanthropy, but, unlike Emmeline's or

Julia's, it provokes unease in the reader rather than admiration or imaginative identification. Mary is the 'slave of compassion', an ascetic who refuses gratification, happy only when suffering through good deeds or when tearfully contemplating her own virtue. The description of her childhood makes benevolence not simply a given, an innate property, but a consequence of lovelessness and isolation, companion to the melancholy reading of Thomson's *Seasons* and Young's *Night Thoughts*. Similarly, although the philanthropy initially results in grateful peasants, Mary later meets only ingratitude in the objects she patronizes, and neither the woman rescued from the ship nor the starving family stricken with putrid fever responds in proper sentimental fashion:

> For some time she had observed that she was not treated with the same respect as formerly; her favours were forgotten when no more were expected. This ingratitude hurt her, as did a similar instance in the woman who came out of the ship. Mary had hitherto supported her; as her finances were growing low, she hinted to her, that she ought to try to earn her own subsistence: the woman in return loaded her with abuse. (p. 85)

Self-pityingly, Mary muses, 'Too well have I loved my fellow creatures: I have been wounded by ingratitude.' In such scenes there is a dispersing of the dream of sentimental fellowship, which becomes problematic when the patron is a solitary woman.

Morality and sensibility

In the early *David Simple* and *Clarissa*, villainy was discovered and labelled; its blackness heightened the whiteness of the sentimental and virtuous protagonists. Instruction could therefore be delivered in some measure by the plot and by the sentiments the characters uttered as they passed along their almost allegorical way. By the late eighteenth century, however, such instruction is no longer provided, for villainy cannot be discerned and labelled. In *Emmeline* the manic and abducting cousin is rather engaging in his impulsiveness and he is easily subdued by the heroine's greater firmness, while in *Mary, A Fiction* the threatening husband proves to be a 'good-natured, weak' young man. *Julia de Roubigné* encloses a piece of straight sentimental instruction, a paper on marriage from the dead mother which declares the duties of a subordinate wife to be 'sweetness of temper, affection to a husband, and attention to his interests'. But the novel as a whole questions this advice since the mother's wifely piety helps create her daughter's disastrous fate.

The instruction on sensibility itself is even more problematic. According to Sir Walter Scott's *Lives of the Novelists*, Mackenzie specifically composed a story

> in which the characters should be all naturally virtuous, and where the calamities of the catastrophe should arise . . . not out of schemes of premeditated villainy, but from the excess and over-indulgence of passions and feelings, in themselves blameless, nay, praiseworthy, but which, encouraged to a morbid excess . . . lead to the most disastrous consequences.[6]

Unlike Richardson, who was eager to impose a single instructional reading on his text, Mackenzie is not clear about what his message is or should be. As he wrote concerning the publication of *Julia de Roubigné*,

> I am every day more & more stumbled about the proper Education of your Sex; there is a bewitching Sensibility we are apt to enourage in them, which I begin to fear is often a very unsafe Guide thro' Life & I am sometimes at Repentance myself, for having done even the little that was in my Power towards it's Encouragement. (27 January 1777)

The man of feeling was never intended as a guide for life, although his responses could be imitated, but the common fear of fiction's power over susceptible females always made relevant the moral tendency of a novel aimed at women.

In *Mary, A Fiction*, the moral tendency of sensibility is even more unclear. Certainly sensibility is desirable and privileged in women:

> [It] is the most exquisite feeling of which the human soul is susceptible; when it pervades us, we feel happy . . . It is this quickness, this delicacy of feeling which enables us to relish the sublime touches of the poet, and the painter; it is this, which expands the soul . . . [and makes it] disposed to be virtuous.

This eulogistic passage became a *locus classicus* of sensibility and was anthologized (together with an extract from Sterne's *A Sentimental Journey*) in *The Young Gentleman & Lady's Instructor* (1809). Yet the praise comes towards the end of a novel that throws grave doubts on the functioning of sensibility in society, and it has a shrill sound, underlined by the stress on the distinguishing superiority which sensibility gives to its devotees, those free from the gratifications of the world and sensuality.

Unlike in Richardson, sensibility seems to dissipate rather than form fellowship, for it separates Mary with a wall of disdain from almost everyone she cannot philanthropically patronize. Indeed it seems to have parted company from earthly community altogether and to function, even more than the Man of Feeling's, solely in heaven, the only realm of real emotion: 'in a state of bliss, it will be the society of beings we can love, without the alloy that earthly infirmities mix with our best affections, that will constitute great part of our happiness' (p. 68). With these 'notions' Mary believes that she must always be a misfit in society, for the 'world' is 'ever hostile and armed against the feeling heart!'

Sensibility here seems divisively individualistic. In addition, its anti-sexual quality, present in *Emmeline* and in *Julia de Roubigné* despite its Rousseauist model, becomes in *Mary, A Fiction* less an underlining of purity that a neurotic recoil. In *The History of Sexuality* Foucault noted that the eighteenth-century silences made sex 'an element that functions alongside the things said'. In *Mary, A Fiction* the worrying at sexuality renders it as audible as the *double entendres* of *Tristram Shandy*. But, although present and feared, sexuality provides no active threat to female purity – it is denied the resonance Lovelace gives it since it derives from a weak, well-meaning man and is within marriage.

Without persecution and social purpose, then, and without extreme sexual threat, female sensibility comes perilously close to the self-indulgence of a wilful victim, with no redemptive influence and no power of cure:

> will light ever break in? . . . Do all suffer like me; or am I framed so as to be particularly susceptible of misery? . . . lie still my throbbing heart, or burst; . . . why do thoughts so rapidly rush into my mind, and yet when they disappear leave such deep traces? I could almost wish for the madman's happiness, and in a strong imagination lose a sense of woe. (*Mary, A Fiction*, pp. 85–6)

Techniques

The tableaux of *Emmeline* are mainly of blissful domesticity, repetitiously constructed for the sensitive voyeur within the text. By the 1780s they are less morally clear than when Sarah Fielding wrote and they have gathered illicit and incestuous overtones. So the hero sees his sister 'to all appearance dead' in the arms of her seducer, with Emmeline pale and lifeless beside her. Another kind of sensationalism creeps into the scenes in the sheer number of postures and relationships; a mother will, for example, be grieving over a dying son who is seen as a father surrogate by a repentant adulteress, who is in turn accepted by the mother as her sister in grief. The proliferation of functions, so that every domestic and emotional possibility is manifest, rather resembles the baroque sexual fantasies of the Marquis de Sade, whose geometric exercises leave nothing untouched.

By 1777, the year of *Julia de Roubigné*, the sentimental novel had so informed consciousness that fictional characters like Sterne's Yorick and the Man of Feeling can be shown using sentimental tableaux to inspire and manipulate themselves into sentimental attitudes. The growing ambivalence of Mackenzie's attitude to sensibility, however, meant that the results of such fiction-inspired manipulation were not always happy. The stern Montauban, for example, sees his beloved not as she is, a young girl lovesick for another, but in terms of a sentimental tableau of domesticity in which she functions 'like our guardian angel, without his superiority'. The result is her destruction. Julia herself begins the process of her fall by making the appeal of her parents irresistible through their transformation into a carefully constructed emotional tableau:

> My mother stood on one side, looking gently upwards, her hands, which were clasped together, leaning on my father's shoulder. He had one hand in his side, the other pressed on his bosom, his figure seeming to rise above itself, and his eye bent steadily forward.—Methought, as I looked on them, I was above the fears of humanity! (*Julia de Roubigné*, p. 47)

Later, deprived of any description of her lover's return, she creates a picture from her own store of sentimental scenes which results in a fatal and overwhelming desire to meet Savillon:

> I see him, I see him now . . . I see him start back in amazement and despair: his eyes wild and haggard, his voice lost in the throb of astonishment! He thinks on the shadow which his fond hopes had reared – the dreams of happiness! Say not that he wept at the

thought – Had those tears fallen upon Julia's grave, memory! thou couldst not thus have stung me. (*Julia de Roubigné*, p. 128)

In the late novels of female sensibility, the repetition so generally common in sentimental fiction works through both action and account. In *Mary, A Fiction* deaths and miseries recur, and in *Emmeline* there are repeated scenes illustrating middle-class crassness and the manic cousin's desire. In *Julia de Roubigné*, there is reiteration of a single affecting incident. Sometimes this is a matter of increasing emotion through incremental accounts, as in *The Man of Feeling* – the scene of the mother's death is given in all its swooning, sobbing and clasping detail first by the maid and then by Julia. But at other times it is a dramatic device, as when Julia describes the moment when she fears her husband has seen her lover's portrait in her possession; the same scene is given from her husband's very different point of view, with the result that the protagonists are emphatically separated rather like the obsessional characters of *Tristram Shandy*. Here, however, there is no outpouring of sentiment to shatter the isolation.

Like Richardson's fiction, the novel of the male sentimental hero is fragmented – *A Sentimental Journey* and *The Man of Feeling* lapse into silence or are seemingly broken in places. In the novel of female sentiment, the letter form similarly allows this fragmentation and *Sidney Bidulph*, for example, breaks into discrete pieces. *Julia de Roubigné* is said to be a translation of letters, some of which have been in whole or part suppressed and whose order is due partly to the translator's indolence. The narrated *Mary, A Fiction* falls into chapters so short that a page comprehends the final one, while the Advertisement boasts that the book is 'an artless tale, without episodes'.

Broken syntax and typographical exuberance mark these novels, especially the epistolary ones, since the lady of feeling must stress her non-verbal sensibility through emphasizing the limited nature of verbal communication. Extra-linguistic gestures are signified by stage directions, often in brackets, by italics, dashes and interrupted utterances. Emotive words such as 'mother', 'child', 'friend' or 'virtue' act as talismans requiring no analysis and halting the discourse: ' "Thank God!" she exclaimed, in a rapturous accent, (as, with a deep sigh, I raised my languid eyes, and turned them mournfully towards her – "she lives! – My Emma! – child of my affections!" – Sobs suppressed her utterance)'[7] The ultimate emotion is inexpressible and language is always genuflecting to the inarticulateness of high sensibility.

In some ways such a mannered style seems an effort to make the '*lively present tense*' manner of *Clarissa*'s Lovelace express not the heady voyeurism and sexual ebullience of a man but the fluctuating sensibility of a woman. But such an attempt is vitiated, for, as Richardson knew, the style in women conveyed impotence and strain rather than power and excitement.

The ending

'If I have endowed the young ladies with a degree of sensibility, that might have exposed them to danger, I flatter myself I have taken the proper means of rescuing them from it by marrying them respectively to the men of their hearts', wrote Richard Cumberland about his novel *Arundel*.[8] The endings of many sentimental novels are sheer fantasy and wish fulfilment in which marriage to 'men of their hearts' inevitably follows danger and misery.

In *Emmeline*, the heroine, like Jane Austen's Emma later, achieves matrimony without the disagreeable transplantation lamented by Mrs Elton. Fellowship is suggested by the inclusion of the sentimental friend. In the fantasy marriage of 'The Two Emilys' the ideal of sociability through sentimental outpourings, so much a feature of Richardson, becomes less of a reciprocity and more of a moral domination of the sentimentally superior. If this consummation proved difficult, female authors like Charlotte Smith and Charlotte Lennox were adept at ridding their plots of unwanted husbands.

In the terms of *Julia de Roubigné* it is difficult to conceive of a fate other than death for the heroine. Unlike the spared lover, she could not travel to the West Indies to humanize commerce and free slaves, and her sensibility would not allow contentment in a loveless marriage. Indeed she has already anticipated her death, for the meeting and parting with Savillon in their old nurse's house provokes the kind of summarizing memory that the fictional dying conventionally experience, while at other times she has consciously longed for oblivion. But, although destroyed by the contradictions that destroyed Rousseau's Julie in *La Nouvelle Héloïse*, Mackenzie's Julia does not experience Julie's Clarissa-like death, with friends and well-wishers crowding round and making of her dying a reconciling, almost redemptive act. At least, however, it borrows some resonance from heaven, and it is not entirely unremarked, for her murdering husband has heard and been softened by the divine music she plays:

> when I was returning to my apartment, I heard the sound of music proceeding from my wife's chambers . . . she sat at the organ, her fingers pressing on the keys, and her look up-raised with enthusiastic rapture! – The solemn sounds still ring in my ear! such as angels might play when the sainted soul ascends to heaven! (*Julia de Roubigné*, p. 153)

The ending of *Mary, A Fiction* has greater difficulties, since there is no obvious narrative progress for the melancholic Mary. Wollstonecraft cannot send her heroine along the reclusive route of the man of feeling, for, where sentimental men might reject or accept society, women always yearned to be a part of it and seemed to exist only tenuously when removed from it. The reclusive female who is not waiting for a man is not a cliché in literature. Since she is already married, marriage cannot be used to attempt a cure for her morbid condition, as for *Grandison's* hysterical Clementina, and the 'sickness' and 'faintness' she feels when her husband mentions love make any valuing of her present tie impossible.

As in *Julia de Roubigné*, then, the alternative to marriage would seem to be death. But, in Wollstonecraft's novel, there are no onlookers. Once the female friend and the hero have gone, Mary is left a 'solitary wretch'. Because of the woman's dependence on society, a lonely death unwitnessed and unheard is denied the power it could have had for a man of feeling and it simply appears as defeat:

> [In her heart] there was a void, that even benevolence and religion could not fill. The latter taught her to struggle for resignation; and the former rendered life supportable.
>
> Her delicate state of health did not promise long life. In moments of solitary sadness, a gleam of joy would dart across her mind—She thought she was hastening to that world *where there is neither marrying*, nor giving in marriage. (*Mary, A Fiction*, p. 111)

This is the truncated end of the novel; the silence of the author about the heroine's future is not the pregnant, emotive silence of sentimental feeling, but her bafflement before the failure of the Richardsonian construction of femininity. The sentimental death hinted at is not even written into the work. Heaven is not the place where sensibility alone enjoys status and meaning, as it is for the exiled man of feeling, nor is it any longer the familial state – 'my father's house' – of the woman of feeling, giving significance to her trials in life. It has become merely a realm without marriage.

The heroic female plot of suffering is untenable without the deep Christian context that Richardson considered essential for his sacrifice of woman. It is also untenable without the solid belief in gender distinctions, vibrating to the significant threat of Lovelace and undisturbed by the existence of invalid men and melancholic women. In Charlotte Smith's late novel, *Desmond* (1792), the works of Richardson become 'soothing tales of imagination', blotting out for a moment the 'hideous realities of human life' (II, p. 148).

VIII   *The Attack on Sensibility*

Sentimentalism was always on the defensive. From the outset it opposed the individualistic and thrusting values that were transforming Britain into an industrial and imperial power. Yet it could not be allied with the cultured, gentlemanly élite, whose members often apprehended it as anodyne, escapist and simplifying, suitable as a mode for a growing mass audience of the semi-literate and for women who were marginal both to the economic and social enterprise and to traditional literary culture.

Sentimental literature expressed its defensiveness directly through its nostalgic visions of harmonious fellowship and virtuous men and women. The former turned out to be either isolationist and in retreat from the metropolitan sources of power or fragile in its contact with the worldly and the predatory; the latter were often reclusive, melancholy or doomed. Although in the philosophy and literature of the early and mid eighteenth century this harmonious fellowship and the image of the sensitive benevolist could present a social and individual ideal, towards the end of the century the ideal disintegrated as the political and psychological implications of sentimental doctrine were clarified and assaulted.

Politics

The fate of sensibility in England is allied to the political situation. In the closing years of the eighteenth century, the English reacted not only to the French Revolution and its aftermath but also to the political and social situation at home. The *Anti-Jacobin Review*, the new organ of conservative opinion, worked to bind sensibility to radicalism, or 'Jacobinism' as it insisted on calling any reformist view, and it blamed both for the unrest it feared was spreading in England. The radicals, on their side, were just as eager as the conservatives to align sensibility with their opponents, and they attacked as sentimental the reactionary nostalgia and emotional callousness they saw promoted in the *Anti-Jacobin*. Clearly neither side wished to be left in possession of a now unfashionable sensibility, but neither side wanted entirely to abandon the power of emotive, sentimental language.

Many of the British supporters of the early French Revolution were rhetorically sentimental, although its radical theorists were far less so. For instance the early revolutionary events and measures were fulsomely depicted by Helen Maria Williams in reports which were much read, for she was one of the few eye-witnesses of what she related. In her lengthy series of letters, she rapturously converted the French ceremonies and revolutionary festivities into enactments of the tableaux of the sentimental fiction she also wrote; French revolutionary policy became crystallized into poignant family relationships and scenes of domestic tenderness.[1] The liberal Major Cartwright responded to French events with the solitary tear of sentimental fiction, the glistening eye and the leaping and ecstatic heart, a response regarded as eccentrically 'whimsical' by conservative critics.[2]

Because of these and many other effusive reports of the Revolution, when large-scale killings began in France under Robespierre it was easy for opponents to implicate sensibility. In a famous cartoon entitled 'New Morality', James Gillray portrayed the figure of Sensibility weeping over a dead bird, with the works of Rousseau in one hand; a foot rests on the unregarded head of Louis XVI. In lines from *The New Morality*, published by William Canning in the last issue of the *Anti-Jacobin* (9 July 1798), 'Sweet Sensibility' is implicated in French crimes through its disordered morality:

> False by degrees, and exquisitely wrong; –
> – For the crushed beetle *first*, – the widow'd dove,
> And all the warbled sorrows of the grove; –
> *Next* for poor suffering *guilt*; and *last* of all,
> For Parents, Friends, a King and Country's fall.

Sensibility is accused of being unmoved by 'foul crimes, but sicklied o'er with freedom's name'.

Under the influence of the Jacobin Terror, former liberals came to believe that indiscriminate benevolence and desire to benefit humanity would lead to malignancy and that the over-warm heart would inevitably grow intolerant. In *Example of France, a Warning to Britain* (1793), Arthur Young blamed sensibility for the belief that what ought to be is or could be, a foolish idea leading directly to the bloodshed and chaos in France.

The long French wars in which Britain was engaged on and off from the early 1790s to 1815 meant a recoiling from revolutionary ideas. They also signalled a retreat from internationalism and from tendencies that seemed to ignore national boundaries. The cult of sensibility that had swept Europe in the 1760s and 1770s and had made Goethe's Werther a household name in literate England, and Clarissa and Yorick familiar presences in Germany and France gave way to a stress on national literature and to qualities considered peculiarly British, such as restraint, self-control and stoical, wry acceptance. The years of most vigorous conservative attack on sensibility – from Jane Austen, Coleridge, and the *Anti-Jacobin* – coincided with the alarmist and military years in England, when sensibility was felt to be demoralizing, anti-Christian and childishly French.

When they wrote their most influential works, the major English radical writers were severely rational. Like their conservative critics, they saw sensibility as dangerous and self-indulgent. It was the mode of an apathetic middle class which enjoyed dabbling in philanthropy, especially when it involved groups far from home, such as African slaves. It did not mount a general attack on the social problems of an unequal and unfree society and it did not encourage political response: indeed, by giving aristocracy and privilege a humane face, as it did in the fictional pictures of semi-feudal harmony, it often reinforced the legitimacy of the ruling classes. In *Pigott's Political Dictionary* (1795) the Rousseauist sentimental festival of social togetherness became a delusion and a confusion exalting folly and sinking talents.

Sensibility, it was often noted, could coexist with social cruelty: 'Where is the dignity, the infallibility, in the fair ladies, whom . . . the captive negroes curse in all the agony of bodily pain, for the unheard of tortures they invent?' asked Mary Wollstonecraft. Pathos and effusions were no remedy for poverty and injustice: 'Such misery demands more than tears'; revolutionary action should not be defused by individual humanitarianism or an idealization of society's victims.[3]

The clearest radical opposition to sensibility as a conservative mode occurs in the pamphlet and book war started by the publication in 1790 of Edmund Burke's *Reflections on the Revolution in France*; the Wollstonecraft quotations above come from the first reply, *A Vindication of the Rights of Men*, which attacked the conservative work for its smug criticism of the French Revolution and its support of the unjust British status quo. Along with Burke's later opponents, a newly anti-sentimental Wollstonecraft considered the language and methods of *Reflections* just as offensive as the opinions, since Burke's defence of the establishment favoured the high sentimental style with chiaroscuro effects and persuasive emotional vignettes of tumbled royalty.

Burke saw himself as a reasonable man, praising 'a manly, moral, regulated liberty', but Wollstonecraft emasculated him by accusing him of the irrationality and effeminacy of sentiment. He was, she claimed, weakly emotional and self-indulgent, viewing the Revolution as a kind of theatrical tragedy, while ignoring the suffering masses out of which it grew. With Paine and Thomas Christie, she believed that he was using his magnificent sentimental language to manipulate the reader into reverence for institutions that deserved only scorn.

Society

By conservatives, sentimental doctrine was judged to be levelling since it evaluated a person not by achievement or breeding but by ability to feel. In William Beckford's *Modern Novel Writing or The Elegant Enthusiast* (1796), the female novel was mocked for its fantasy of aristocratic marriage as an escape from 'plebeian vulgarity'; none the less, fiction – and especially drama – did make heroes and heroines of the middling classes and put forward ideals that were familial and domestic, within the reach of everyone, rather than intellectual and discriminating. Sensibility appeared to favour reform by its emphasis on life's victims, and to question, if not attack, the established hierarchies of birth and gender.

The emphasis on the lower orders could become an affectation in those unlikely to diminish their own highness and privilege; the pose was lightly mocked by Edward Gibbon in his *Autobiography*:

> Mr. d'Alembert relates that, as he was walking in the gardens of Sans Souci with the King of Prussia, Frederick said to him, 'Do you see that old woman, a poor weeder, asleep on that sunny bank? She is probably a more happy being than either of us.'
>
> The king and the philosopher may speak for themselves; for my part, I do not envy the old woman . . . . My nerves are not tremblingly alive, and my literary temper is so happily framed that I am less sensible of pain than of pleasure.[4]

The classically educated minority, often connected by inclination if not always by birth to the ruling establishment, men such as Johnson, Sheridan and Gibbon, saw sensibility undermining classical standards and diffusing the centralized authority of London, the court and the universities. The poetry and fiction of sensibility in the last part of the century often issued from the provinces, where circulating libraries dealing in Gothic and sentimental novels were mushrooming.[5] Popular and élitist taste moved further apart, and the sentimental strain was associated firmly with the under-educated, the ill-bred and the non-metro-politan. Jane Austen's Lucy Steele of *Sense and Sensibility*, who speaks vulgar jargon and displays sentimental attitudes, comes from Plymouth, where her uncle tutors boys for a living; she is in want of 'delicacy, of rectitude, and of integrity of mind'. When Sheridan mocked sentimental drama, a reviewer worried that his mockery would be 'too refined for the Multitude' who wept at such plays.

Sensibility was also of course associated with women, who, denied the classical education of the universities, were reading and writing sentimental novels and poems in ever-increasing numbers. To many in Britain the cult of sensibility seemed to have feminized the nation, given women undue prominence, and emasculated men. The archetypal man of feeling created by Mackenzie, Sterne and Goethe came to seem effete and sexually enervated or dishonest. Sometimes he was even repudiated by his creator. The older Goethe prefixed verses to later editions of *The Sorrows of Young Werther* which included the line: 'Be a man and do not follow me.' In a *Lounger* essay (18 June 1785), Mackenzie attacked what he regarded as the French version of sensibility for its possible substitution of visionary feeling for practical duties, but he could not avoid criticism of his own *Man of Feeling* in the process: 'This separation of conscience from feeling is a depravity of the most pernicious sort', for it destroys obligations to virtue and allows a person 'pride in his own delicacy'.

Beyond the fear of sensibility's emasculating effect on men, there continued widespread anxiety at the social result of fictional sensibility on women. Presumably because of their vapid lives, their weak heads and their greater susceptibility, which allowed them to be both more virtuous and more vulnerable, women, it was surmised, might start to live through fantasy and so avoid becoming devoted wives and practical mothers. The fear had been expressed from the outset of the sentimental tendency, for as early as Defoe's *The Family Instructor* (1715) women were regarded as far more at risk from fantasy than men; the tract portrays erring children of both sexes, but only the daughter must burn her reading matter to reform.

The fear of fiction's effect on women's lives was especially articulated when the novel became the dominant form. At first the assault had been on French romance, but later it switched to seemingly more realistic British fiction. In 1677 *The Ladies Calling* attacked romance as pernicious for young women who were created to work in the real world, while in 1719, in *Love in Excess*, Eliza Haywood admitted that fiction prepared the reader's mind for 'Amorous Impressions'. In the 1760s, Charlotte Lennox's *The Female Quixote* painted a misguided heroine expecting knightly codes to obtain in modern times; George Colman the Elder in *Polly Honeycombe* (1760) pictured a fiction-reading miss trying to fashion life into a novel. Samuel Johnson attacked fiction's power over the young, the ignorant and the idle, the last two groups no doubt including a majority of women (*Rambler*, 31 March 1750).

Stories abounded of fiction-maddened girls panting to marry servants. In the early part of the century, they mistook them for princes in disguise (Jane Barker, 1726), but in later years they judged menials their equals in sensibility, which could be possessed as well by a footman as by a lord (Richard Berenger, 1754). The earlier romance-inflicted girl was usually allowed to come to her senses: 'It was such Romantic Whimsies that brought upon me the Ruin and Distress in which you behold me; I had read Plays, Novels and Romances'. The novel-reading girl is, however, often ruined for life, turned into a spinsterly sentimental addict.

The discourse of courtship and female flattery associated with sensibility marked women's economic decline and lessened power within marriage. The danger of the situation inhered in the stark opposition of fiction and reality: the sentimental elevation of the maiden or mother on the one hand and the possibly brutal reality of female economic and social impotence within marriage on the other. As early as 1739, the author of *The Present State of Matrimony* expressed the problem, which was often reiterated: 'Yesterday she was assured by her Lover, that his Life depended on her's . . . But as soon as the Parson has pronounced the fatal Words, he puts on the Lord and Master'.[6] Sentimental fiction supplied the fantasy that intensified the shock of marriage, as well as providing the escape once a woman had 'dwindled into a wife'.

Sensibility also fared badly with those wishing to improve women's position in society. While through fiction it delivered a needed wish-fulfilment of power, it also obscured women's actual impotence, and it prevented practical and limited reform. The fiction of Mary Wollstonecraft shows her gradually realizing this fact. In *Mary, A Fiction* in 1788 she endorsed her sentimental heroine despite Mary's evident self-pity and indulgence in the 'luxury of doing good'. Already, however, Wollstonecraft reproves Mary's mother for reading novels, 'those most delightful substitutes for bodily dissipation'. A decade later in *The Wrongs of Woman* (1798) she portrays a heroine imprisoned in a madhouse by the husband she sentimentally chose; whilst under the influence of another romantic passion and of Rousseau's sentimental fiction, she adapts to her prison setting and ceases to struggle. In *A Vindication to the Rights of Woman* (1792), her most sustained attack on sensibility, Wollstonecraft insists on severe rationality as the basis of reform for women: 'soft phrases, susceptibility of heart, delicacy of sentiment, and refinement of taste, are almost synonymous with epithets of weakness . . . those beings who are only the objects of pity . . . will soon become objects of contempt.'[7]

In *Madness and Civilization* Foucault sums up the eighteenth-century fear of the effect of fiction and fictional sensibility on women:

The novel constitutes the milieu of perversion *par excellence*, of all sensibility; it detaches the soul from all that is immediate and natural in feeling and leads it into an imaginary world of sentiments violent in proportion to their unreality, and less controlled by the gentle laws of nature. 'The existence of so many authors has produced a host of readers, and continuous reading generates every nervous complaint; perhaps of all causes that have harmed women's health, the principal one has been the unfortunate multiplication of novels in the last hundred years . . . a girl who at ten reads instead of running will, at twenty, be a woman with the vapors and not a good nurse' (quoted from *Gazette salutaire* 6 October 1768).[8]

As the eighteenth century closed, sensibility was viewed more and more as anti-community, a progressing away from, not into, Humean social sympathy. Seeming profoundly separatist, it veered from politics and came to assert the individual's right to, for example, sexual freedom and unfamilial relationships, in opposition to the institution of Christian marriage. So in Shelley's *Revolt of Islam* the Rousseauist communal rituals of Helen Maria Williams's French Revolution are enacted but prove impotent, and the ideal is discovered not in the social sphere but in the imaginative capacities of individuals. Meanwhile the central pair of lovers – brother and sister in the original version – form a kind of parody of the familial-social order of sentimentalism as their fraternal relationship becomes erotic and incestuous. The final posture in Shelley's poem is close to the isolation of the graveyard poets, but it is not an escape on behalf of a religious or quasi-religious realm, as in Young and Gray, but a retreat from direct hope in sentimental fellowship to an unsentimental belief in the power of the single human mind.

Like other first-generation Romantic poets, originally far closer to the poets of sensibility than their successors, William Blake felt the attraction of communal ritual in society, the aesthetic charity of the feats and processions in, for example, 'Holy Thursday' of *Songs of Innocence*. In the companion 'Holy Thursday' of *Songs of Experience*, however, the reciprocal sympathy of the Humean vision that was caught in Rousseauist ritual is transformed into an enactment of domination and submission, and the paternalistic simply becomes the patriarchal. The communal world of sensibility is, in Blakean terms, merely Beulah, the innocent uncomplicated realm to be intellectually transcended by each individual.

Morality

'Manners change from generation to generation, and with manners morals appear to change', wrote Coleridge. By the last decades of the eighteenth century, sensibility was felt to have done its work and to have moved manners from coarseness towards gentility; in the process it was judged to have softened or undermined morals as well. The attack on sensibility as immoral or amoral came from all quarters, from the evangelical Christian Hannah More, from the atheist Marquis de Sade, from the politically conservative Coleridge and from the radical anarchist Godwin.

Perhaps the most frequent charge was that it weakened Christian standards and morality. Thomas Rowlandson engraved a series of illustrations called *The Man of Feeling* in which the hero's Christian benevolent interest in young women became sexual rather than sentimental. Hannah More, who had once offered poetic praise to sensibility, came to see it as a flight from responsibility, since a feeling heart could justify inaction and excuse error. Suffering, she insisted, was not an aesthetic experience aimed at a spectator, nor a blameless condition with no cause, as sentimentalists so often implied; instead it was the result of sin and human fallibility. Life was not given to gratify sensation but 'to be useful to others'.

Together with many other women moralists, Hannah More saw sensibility striking at the Christian notion of female chastity. In the early years, sensibility had mythologized and hugely elevated a flamboyant virginity in the young girl, but, as the decades proceeded, the emphasis on instinct and love seemed to have grown with the stress on spontaneity. Fictional heroines who indulged sexually usually died indeed; none the less they remained heroines and their surrender to irrational and uncontrolled passion often appeared fascinating and noble. As early as *Pamela Censured* in 1741 and *Critical Remarks* in 1754 it was noted that, although Richardson aimed at virtue, yet the novels, in describing 'the endearments between the sexes', actually promoted passion and heightened and inflamed the senses. A review of Richard Cumberland's *Arundel* in the *Analytical Review* (III, January–April 1789), probably by Mary Wollstonecraft, claimed that novels could inspire in girls 'false notions and hopes, teach them affectation, and shake their principles by representing love as irresistible, love at first sight'.

By the later 1790s the *Anti-Jacobin* made sensibility synonymous with un–Christian sexual licence in women. Ironically one of its main exemplars was Mary Wollstonecraft, whose unmarried loves and illegitimate child came to eclipse her anti-sentimental opinions. Both Hannah More and Mary Wollstonecraft in *A Vindication of the Rights of Woman* based their analysis not on an ideal of society but on society as it was. Since chastity was required for women to flourish socially, then sexual licence became a trap for them; in Wollstonecraft's phrase, it was a collusion by women in the 'libertine reveries of men'. Sexuality for Maria Edgeworth in *Letters for Literary Ladies* was a 'wayward power' which erased the 'boundaries of right and wrong' and obscured the reality of society. A refusal by women to see society as it was actually constructed could only lead to unhappiness; in Edgeworth's view, obfuscating sensibility leading to sexuality was not only wrong for women but also deeply unwise.

In France the Marquis de Sade devastatingly connected female sentimental attitudes with male sexual desire. His seductive and vulnerable Justine is virtue in distress; she is a lady who brims with sensibility and who forms delicious tableaux of titillating misery. Female passivity and tenderness, Sade insisted, far from inspiring male benevolence and care, actually provoked 'sadistic' violence and sexual violation – a fact which the sentimental novel from *Clarissa* onwards largely confirmed.

Like the connection between sensibility and cruelty, the line between sensibility and suicide was not lost on critics. The exaltation of Wertherian death is mocked by Thomas Love Peacock in *Nightmare Abbey*, where his hero at the last minute decides not to kill himself for disappointed love like Werther, but to drink up the family Madeira instead.

Given the imperfections of the world and the lack of discrimination in which sensibility gloried, sentimentalists, if they survived, would be likely to achieve misery as often as pleasure since they would be constantly wounded by the unkindness of others. This point is neatly made in the centre of an actual sentimental novel which yet purports to be a warning against sensibility: Mary Hays's *Memoirs of Emma Courtney* (1796), in which she included not only her own miserable love-letters, but also the correspondence with the rationalist Godwin, who counselled her in her unhappy affair.

In her own letters, the heroine glories in her sensibility and benevolence despite her sorry progress in life, and she bewails the fact that others, especially men, neither share nor appreciate these qualities. Godwin as Mr Francis, however, argues that, since society and its institutions are imperfect, reasonless benevolence is an inappropriate response to life and will lead to disillusion. Along with any other organ, the heart, so much appealed to as the last court in sentimental writing, should be investigated; miseries should be examined, not welcomed, since the majority would probably be judged self-inflicted.

For Godwin, sensibility was the decadence of civilization, a 'moon-struck madness, hunting after torture'; it was the result of too much leisure in the higher classes, a species of 'folly begotten upon fastidious indolence'. In the end, too, it could lead to vice as well as despair. To illustrate his point, in 1805 he rewrote Mackenzie's *Man of Feeling* as *Fleetwood: or, The New Man of Feeling*, in which the sentimental man grows vicious through sheer lack of opportunity for virtue.

Political Justice (1793) contains Godwin's alternative vision, incorporating aspects of sentimentalism but utterly rejecting others. Its concern is obviously political but, since the formerly Dissenting Godwin saw politics as an extension of ethics, it also treats morality and the nature of virtue.

The work follows some of the tendencies of sentimental morality. The hedonism that lies latent in Shaftesbury's philosophy comes to the fore; pleasure is desirable and pain the only evil. This Hutchesonian utilitarian streak overwhelms other aspects of senti-mental philosophy, and utility – albeit in a rather indirect form, since one pursues the happiness of others through rationally enlightening them – becomes the prime concern of ethics and social organization. The subjective context of an action, so important in sentimentalism, figures only in so far as it suggests a 'continuation of benefit or injury', and on the whole rational action and result supersede sentimental intention and response.

Although in later editions of *Political Justice*, in 1796 and 1798, Godwin continues the sentimental belief in benevolence as the greatest source of pleasure and follows Shaftesbury and Hume in appreciating compassion and sympathy, in each edition he utterly opposes the sentimental privileging of feeling over all other faculties. Assuming with Shaftesbury that humanity is endowed with good impulses, he yet argues strenuously against the idea of innate principles and instinctive morality. Sentimental virtue derives from an outpouring of sympathy aroused by a particular spectacle, but for Godwin this kind of virtue is mere self-indulgence. Real virtue must consist in disinterested concern for the welfare of society, now seen more as the large stratified nation than as the small familial fellowship of Humean sentimentalism. Society will not be improved by little hierarchical rituals but by a gradual movement upwards of the lower orders.

In place of sentimental response and individual action, Godwin emphasizes duty which will be discovered not through feeling but through reason. Here he parts company most completely with sentimental philosophy, for his way forward politically and ethically is through reason's regulation of emotion: 'It is to the improvement of reason . . . that we are to look for the improvement of our social condition.'[9] The evanescent moods and physical emanations of sensibility resulting in momentary tearful compassion have no staying power and no ability to improve society at large. In Germany Kant's rigorous divorcing of emotion from morality was similar in effect to Godwin's system in its undermining of sentimentalism's philosophical basis.

A very differently expressed attack on sensibility was mounted by Coleridge, who was as eager as Godwin to sever sensibility from benevolence and humanitarianism. His eagerness sprang, however, not from a belief in a superior rational system but in part from a deeply gendered apprehension of human psychology, an apprehension shared to some extent by Godwin who, although much admiring his wife Mary Wollstonecraft, associated her with sensibility and himself with rationality when he came to write her biography. Coleridge used the common abusive gender terms for sensibility, terming it effeminacy and emasculation. Sensibility was female, unstrenuous, anti-social and self-indulgent, a physical manipulation and a sensation of the body. The sensation was felt by men and women alike, but was especially associated with the selfish, effeminate side of the personality which, in men, needed proper and manly curbs.

Sensibility in its selfish and self-regarding form had nothing to do with moral and social reform, and Coleridge echoes Mary Wollstonecraft's point that literary female sensibility need not even be benevolent. The image of the weeping lady reader, so moving to the young Wordsworth, became the summary of self-indulgent feeling:

She sips a beverage sweetened with human blood, even while she is weeping over the refined sorrows of Werther and Clementina. Sensibility is not Benevolence. Nay, by making us tremblingly alive to trifling misfortunes, it frequently prevents it and induces effeminate and cowardly selfishness. (*The Watchman*, 25 March 1796)

In *Aids to Reflection*, written over a quarter of a century later, sentimentalists once again avert their gaze from suffering in the world and reveal effeminate, selfish and cowardly hearts, pampered with feelings too delicate for use; they 'shun the wretched' while sighing for abstract wretchedness, and they nurse 'in some delicious solitude/ their slothful loves and dainty sympathies'.

For Coleridge, the evil of the 'sentimental philosophy of Sterne, and his numerous imitators' surpassed that of Hobbes and the materialists which it aimed to refute. It justified the most violent and vicious appetites as irresistible feeling and tender sensibility. Reason, law and duty clarify, but sensibility, amoral and passive, exists in 'the twilight between vice and virtue'.

Literature

From the 1780s onwards, sentimental literature and the principles behind it were bombarded with criticism and ridicule. German theorists like Friedrich Schlegel, Novalis and Schelling challenged their extreme emotionalism and insisted on aesthetic considerations, in a way returning to Shaftesbury who, before the heady days of the cult of sensibility, had emphasized aesthetic education. Schlegel sought a tragic art that would toughen and strengthen the mind by producing complicated and difficult conflicts. Sentimental works, he thought, had softened the soul; with their immediate reference to self, they were too easily consumed. Sentimental drama was accused of provoking 'effeminate tenderness' instead of 'masculine tragic pity'. In place of a criticism of enthusiastic response, Romantic critics emphasized the need for decoding the meaning of a work; the stance of the critic should not be sentimental absorption but detached, ironic self-consciousness. Reading should become a development in self-knowledge, not an education in feeling.

The attacks on sentimental literature fell on all genres and exhibited some common themes. In moral terms the complaint was of degeneration and decay and in gender terms, as suggested by the critical theorists, it was of effeminacy. Drama attracted a good deal of abuse. In *The Critic* Sheridan mocked the sentimental theatre of 'Embraces and Groans, Vows and Prayers, florid Pathos, whining Heroism'. The Prologue lamented the passing of the 'gay days of wickedness and wit' and the dramatic dullness of the 'Far chaster times'. Drama had become 'an arrant prude', retailing 'nightly to the yawning pit,/ The purest morals, undefil'd by wit!' In 'Laughing and Sentimental Comedy' Goldsmith mocked the sentimental idea of reforming society through the stage, echoing Fielding who had made his Tom Jones ridicule the virtuous puppet show.

In the twentieth century, when the taste is for the ironic and self-reflexive in literature, the impossibility of ironic interpretation makes the method of sentimental drama repellant. Characters stating their exemplariness become ridiculous and, acting in a plot, they seem opportunistic and smug. The emphasis of sentimental drama on the parent and child seems less an exemplary statement of social sympathy than an expression of marginality and coercion. Consequently, few modern critics have a good word for that 'perpetual embarrassment', sentimental drama.[10] The historian of the theatre Allardyce Nicoll accepts the first half of the eighteenth century as a 'period of decay and disintegration' and Arthur Sherbo begins a study devoted to sentimental drama by sternly judging it 'a debased literary genre, incapable of producing literature of any marked degree of excellence . . . it is artificial; it exaggerates and distorts human nature and emotion; and it is conceived in terms of a view of life which is absolutely inconsistent with reality'.[11]

The poetry of sensibility is similarly served. With T. S. Eliot, F. R. Leavis dismissed the writers inhabiting the swamps between the Augustan and Romantic heights as 'meditative Miltonizing' writers, and D. J. Enright echoes the contempt: 'Between the self-assured work of the Augustans and the energetic and diverse movements of the Romantic Revival came a period of half-hearted, characterless writing'; he complained of the 'tedium of reading poets who roll in the trough between two creative waves'.[12] Even the poetic period was, until Northrop Frye rechristened it the 'Age of Sensibility', labelled in a peculiarly negative way as 'pre-Romantic'.[13]

With perhaps more Oedipal justification, this scathing attitude was anticipated by the Romantic writers who accused their sentimental predecessors of purposeless and solipsistic self-consciousness. Considering their own self-consciousness as a means of empathizing with the outside world, Keats and Hazlitt felt that the poets of sensibility explored not what it felt like to be another person or object, but what it felt like to be looking at a person or object and how such looking affirmed their own sensibility. Sentimental poets were prisoners of their private selves and consequently divorced from the nature they intended to describe; the sentimental genius became not the primitive poet instinctively in harmony with the world but a constructed literary type, self-conscious, alienated and inadequate. Because of the inadequacy of the poets, the sentimental mode lacked self-confidence, commitment and originality; it appeared clichéd in language and derivative in form.

Steeped in the literature of sensibility, Coleridge in particular, engaged with it constantly in his poetry. In a sonnet quoted in *Biographia Literaria*, he used the affected language of sensibility to mock its egoism: '[I] *mused me* on the *wretched ones* that pass/ O'er the bleak heath of sorrow. But alas!/Most of *myself* I thought!'[14] In his last major poem 'Dejection' sentimental images and themes rise to disturb his mind. The image of the wind instrument as spontaneous inspiration, so much extolled and exploited by poets of sensibility, here becomes ominous, with its implications of unstable power, while the poem questions the plight and value of the withdrawn poet. Like the female poets of sensibility, middle-class male poets from the provinces such as Coleridge felt on the margins of culture and society, and worried about the social insignificance of poetic pain.

Blake and Wordsworth share many of the anti-rational, experiential assumptions of sensibility, but they both flee from its moral instructional aim. The stock characters of sentiment become enigmatic in Wordsworth's *Lyrical Ballads* and the sentimental situations of victim and abandoned woman refuse to yield clear moral generalizations. The works become equivocal rather than univocal and there is little of Richardson's restless worrying after their control. In Blake, moral values are less mocked than mystified and rendered unstable. Pity, for example, in *Songs of Innocence and Experience* remains in one view a virtue, moving towards the reciprocal sympathy of the Humean vision; in another it is the consequence of inequality and domination. The constructed nature of the whole sentimental scheme is stressed, as well as the absurdity of becoming imprisoned within its assumptions. 'Moral Virtues do not Exist; they are Allegories & dissimulations', Blake wrote, and he commented on the pessimism that sentimental belief seems so often to imply: 'Rousseau thought Men Good by Nature: he found them Evil & found no friend.' In his prophetic books, he comes close to articulating the despair of the poet of sensibility in the Spectre of Urthona, whose 'Dark tears' run down his shadowy face: 'knowing/ And seeing life, yet living not. How can I then behold/ And not tremble?'[15] The Victorians kept up the contempt. In an essay of 1857, 'Worldliness and Other Worldliness: The Poet Young', George Eliot dismissed Young's concerns as insincere, his style as ejaculatory and his religion as 'egoism turned heavenward'.

Inevitably, the novel received most of the contemporary abuse of sensibility. Works such as *The Curse of Sentiment* (1787) and *The Illusions of Sentiment* (1788) appeared throughout the 1780s and 1790s and it became almost obligatory to rail against that 'most fatal poison', whatever the author actually constructed in the novel. The effect is often decidedly schizophrenic. Clear sentimentalists degrade sentiment, and sentimental novelists claim not to be writing sentimental novels. For example, Ann Radcliffe in *The Mysteries of Udolpho* warns against the sensibility that is the salient characteristic of her heroine; she does so in a dying speech from a father who has first wiped away his single tear. By the 1790s almost all serious novelists noted the selfishness, irrationality and amorality of the cult of sensibility. Novel after novel claimed it was not a novel and showed characters (usually female) ruined by too much sentiment or the rash perusal of Rousseau.

One of the most sustained attacks on the female sentimental novel came from Jane Austen, all of whose works, from the juvenile parodies to the final unfinished *Sanditon*, form part of the debate of sentimentalism. In her novels the clichés of sentimental fiction are overturned: mothers are vulgar and limited, sentimental friends are a sham, and orphans prove not noble but lower middle class. Families exist not as images of harmonious society, infused with sentimental female values, but as constricting forces, embarrassments to the few sensible offspring they produce. Heroines do not fight against their fathers to marry beyond their power, but choose as spouses paternal men who have helped to bring them up and who are often already within the family. *Sense and Sensibility*, which, in the stories of Marianne and the shadowy Elizas, comes close to invoking the *Clarissa* plot, mocks and stifles the agony of the female victim; ultimately it socializes the near scream of Marianne into sensible rational discourse.[16]

The sentimental style and methods are equally ridiculed in Austen's pages, especially in the juvenilia. She parodies the ecstatic tone of sensibility, which finds the world either amazingly horrid or infinitely superior, and she mocks characters who are over-whelmed by their sensitive and palpitating bodies. Tableaux in all the novels are spurious, often consciously created for effect; looking at them leads not to virtue or Adam Smith's imaginative exchange but simply to error.

The change in serious fiction by women represented by Jane Austen was noticed by Sir Walter Scott who, according to Thackeray, was himself responsible for killing the female senti-mental novel. In his review of *Emma* in 1815, Scott wrote:

A style of the novel has arisen within the last fifteen or twenty years, differing from the former in the points upon which the interest hinges; neither alarming our credulity nor amusing our imagination by wild variety of incident, or by those pictures of romantic affections and sensibility which were formerly as certain attributes of fictitious characters as they are of rare occurrence among those who actually live and die. The substitute for these excitements . . . was the art of copying from nature as she really exists in common walks of life, and presenting to the reader, instead of the splendid scenes of an imaginary world, a correct and striking representation of that which is daily taking place around him. (*Quarterly Review*, 1815, 192–3)

The assault on the sentimental novel written by men was made in terms similar to those deployed against poetry: it was solipsistic and unvirile, 'do-me-good, lack-a-daisical, whining make-believe' in Hazlitt's terms. Coleridge felt his own age superior to the sentimental years because it had a '*mannerly* manliness of taste', a robustness that could accommodate feeling without effeminacy. Nothing 'manly' could come from sensibility which was shapeless and brutish, he thought.

With his mingling of pathos and whimsical humour, Sterne seemed especially distressing, although in his self-conscious chron-icling of inner and outer worlds he remained admired. Coleridge spoke of his 'stupid lechery' and his 'sort of *knowingness*' which implicated the reader in its childish regression and effeminate appeal. Thackeray was repelled by Sterne's deliberate manipulation of emotion – 'he is always looking in my face, watching his effect' – and his indecent exposure of his own feelings:

> A perilous trade, indeed, is that of a man who has to bring his tears and laughter, his recollections, his personal griefs and joys, his private thoughts and feelings to market, to write them on paper, and sell them for money. Does he exaggerate his grief, so as to get his reader's pity for a false sensibility? . . . Where did the lie begin, and did he know where? and where did the truth end in the art and scheme of this man of genius, this actor, this quack?[17]

For the later F. R. Leavis, Sterne's novels were an intricate obscenity, an example of 'irresponsible (and nasty) trifling'.[18]

Despite grudging admiration, Coleridge faulted the hot, day-dreamy, 'vile' and 'oozy' effect of the sentimental Richardson and supported instead the breeziness of Fielding, Thackeray's 'manly' author. Mackenzie fared worst of all. When she was 14, Lady Louisa Stuart dreaded that she would not cry enough at *The Man of Feeling* 'to gain the credit of proper sensibility', but by 1826 the young audience to whom she read the novel laughed at the touches she 'used to think so exquisite'.[19] Writing in 1930, Aldous Huxley found the work 'not merely vulgar, but positively ludicrous . . . vulgar to the point of ridiculousness'.[20]

IX *Epilogue*

The sentimental strain did not die in 1800 but continued into the nineteenth and twentieth centuries, especially in the popular genres of drama and fiction. In English theatre it seems to have tumbled a class into Victorian melodrama. In this the usual schematic characterization of virtue and vice, the central pure victim, the tableaux, the audience exploitation, and the conventionally bombastic diction joined with heightening music and the sensational elements from late eighteenth-century German drama, so that the sentimental set-pieces of suffering domesticity could become, for example 'a picture of domestic agony, a frantic wife, and a poor unconscious infant, in the stern group of the executioners'.[1] In more attenuated form, the sentimental strain in the theatre continued its work of undermining classical modes and genres, ultimately helping to prepare the way for the modern drama of Ibsen and Strindberg.

In the novels of Dickens, Thackeray and George Eliot, the investigation of emotion and the concern for rhetorical manipulation continued, while the Richardsonian emotional didacticism recurred in, for example, D. H. Lawrence's work; *Lady Chatterley's Lover* promotes the novel as the guide and teacher of 'sympathetic consciousness', revealing 'the *passional* secret places of life' where 'the tide of sensitive awareness needs to ebb and flow, cleansing and freshening'.[2] But on the whole critically privileged Victorian fiction moved formally and thematically away from the eighteenth-century sentimental novel. Ideas of special female sensitivity were interrogated and often abandoned, although the notion of the natural moral superiority of woman continued. The serious novel centring on a woman tended to avoid images of female passivity and purity and instead investigated the theme adumbrated by Mary Wollstonecraft, of the gifted woman struggling against a hostile society. Meanwhile, the man of feeling assumed a less debilitated posture in fiction, as he did in Romantic poetry, and embraced and suffered an estranging isolation without benevolence or heaven as cause and consolation. The epistolary form, denying authorial judgement, gave way to the omniscient narrative voice that hindered self-indulgence and unmediated displays of sensibility and allowed a multiplicity of responses.

Yet the movement from sentiment was not wholly a gain, since it denied traditionally sentimental topics close investigation and, following the association of sensibility with effeminacy, made the sentimental style possible only as a lapse from 'masculine' rigour and moral and social seriousness. Consequently the sentimental passages of Thackeray and Dickens have a mawkishness or an embarrassment quite foreign to Richardson's novels or even those of Mackenzie.

Throughout the nineteenth century and indeed into the twentieth century – Alice Walker's *Color Purple* is a recent example – sentimental elements remained most firmly entrenched in the popular novel. In the Gothic-sentimental fiction of Ann Radcliffe's followers, sentiment tended to become sensational, and aspects of the Richardsonian novel entered a fantastic world of innocence and shadowy terror, located far from Jane Austen's 'midland counties of England'. In the domestic novel, especially the extremely successful version by American women, so much resented by Melville, Twain and Hawthorne, many of the clichés of eighteenth-century sensibility recurred. They included the *Clarissa* plot of pure female death, suffered now in even more asexual splendour by the pre-pubescent child, whose body was further purified by consumption. If one ignores Dickens's Little Nell, a creation of sentimentality and unsupported by a Christian and philosophical context, probably the most famous exponent of this plot is Harriet Beecher Stowe's Eva in *Uncle Tom's Cabin* (1852). Her public and redemptive but politically impotent death is enacted in the overcharged language of sensibility:

> The child lay panting on her pillows, as one exhausted, – the large clear eyes rolled up and fixed. Ah, what said those eyes, that spoke so much of heaven! Earth was past, and earthly pain; but so solemn, so mysterious, was the triumphant brightness of that face, that it checked even the sobs of sorrow. They pressed around her, in breathless stillness.
>
> 'Eva,' said St Clare, gently.
>
> She did not hear.
>
> 'O, Eva, tell us what you see, What is it?' said her father.
>
> A bright, a glorious smile passed over her face, and she said, brokenly, – 'O! love, – joy, –peace!' gave one sigh and passed from death into life![3]

Depending on period and personality, readers of such prose can join Godwin and Coleridge in lamenting the prestige of feeling in culture, or they can with Doris Lessing's character in *The Sentimental Agents of the Volyen Empire* (1983) see such flamboyant sensibility as a destabilizing addiction and a glamorous corruption; they can turn away in embarrassment or they can choke and cry.

Notes

I Introduction

1 Henry Mackenzie, *The Man of Feeling* (New York: Norton, 1958), p. 69.

2 Jean François Marmontel, *Poétique françoise* (1763; Johnson Reprints Corporation, 1972), II, pp. 147–8.

3 Erik Erämetsä, 'A study of the word "sentimental" and of other linguistic characteristics of eighteeenth-century sentimentalism in England', *Annales Academiae Scientiarum Fennicae*, Ser. B (Helsinki, 1951). For further remarks on the vocabulary of sensibility, see Walter Francis Wright, *Sensibility in English Prose Fiction 1760–1814. A Reinterpretation* (New York: Russell & Russell, 1937), and Edith Birkhead's 'Sentiment and sensibility in the eighteenth-century novel', *Essays and Studies*, XI, 1925, pp. 2–111.

4 Sir Leslie Stephen, *History of English Thought in the Eighteenth Century* (London: Smith, Elder & Co., 1902), II, p. 436.

5 James Hervey, 'Meditations among the Tombs', *Meditations and Contemplations* (1746; Bungay: C. Brightly and T. Kinnersley, 1807).

6 *The Correspondence of Samuel Richardson*, ed. Anna Laetitia Barbauld (London: Richard Phillips, 1804), IV, pp. 282–3.

7 Among many studies describing the distinction, A. O. Lovejoy's 'On the discrimination of Romanticisms', *PMLA*, XXXIX, pp. 229–53, which separates naturalistic sensibility from transcendental Romanticism, still remains one of the most useful.

II Historical Background

1 John Shebbeare, *Letters on the English Nation* (London, 1755), II, p. 39.

2 Ann Radcliffe, *The Italian* (London: Oxford University Press, 1968), p. 405.

3 *Boswell's Life of Johnson* ed. George Birkbeck Hill (Oxford: Clarendon Press, 1964), V, p. 305.

4 *Satirical Poems Published Anonymously by William Mason with Notes by Horace Walpole*, ed. Paget Toynbee (Oxford: Clarendon Press, 1926), p. 43.

5 H. J. Habakkuk, 'Marriage settlements in the eighteenth century', *Transactions of the Royal Historical Society*, XXXII, 1949, pp. 15–30.

6 Christopher Hill, 'Sex, marriage and the family in England', review article in *Economic History Review*, XXXI, 1978, pp. 450–63.

7 Samuel Richardson, *Sir Charles Grandison* (London: Oxford University Press, 1972), II, p. 355.

8 Michel Foucault, *Madness and Civilization* (London: Tavistock, 1967), pp. 153–4.

9 *Selections from the Tatler and the Spectator*, ed. Angus Ross (Harmondsworth: Penguin, 1982), pp. 209, 156, 252.

10 *Critical Review*, 2nd ser, V, June 1792, p. 132.

11 Thomas Hobbes, *Leviathan*, ed. A. R. Waller (Cambridge: Cambridge University Press, 1904), p. 63.

12 For a useful selection, see *The Cambridge Platonists*, ed. Gerald R. Cragg (New York: Oxford University Press, 1968).

13 John Locke, *An Essay Concerning Human Understanding*, ed. P. H. Nidditch (Oxford: Clarendon Press, 1975), p. 708.

14 *The Life, Unpublished Letters, and Philosophical Regimen of Anthony, Earl of Shaftesbury*, ed. Benjamin Rand (London: Swan Sonnenschein, 1900), p. 403.

15 Anthony Ashley Cooper, third Earl of Shaftesbury, *Character-istics of Men, Manners, Opinions, Times etc.* (London, 1714). For a provocative discussion of the debates of Shaftesbury and Mandeville, see the first four chapters of Martin Price, *To the Palace of Wisdom: Studies in Order and Energy from Dryden to Blake* (Carbondale: Southern Illinois University Press, 1964).

16 David Hume, *A Treatise of Human Nature*, ed. L. A. Selby-Bigge (Oxford: Clarendon Press, 1888), p. 470; *Enquiries concerning the Human Understanding and concerning the Principles of Morals*, ed. L. A. Selby-Bigge (Oxford: Clarendon Press, 1966), p. 231.

17 Adam Smith, *An Inquiry into the Nature and Causes of the Wealth of Nations*, ed. R. H. Campbell and A. S. Skinner (Oxford: Clarendon Press, 1976), p. 27.

18 Edmund Burke, *A Philosophical Enquiry into the Origin of our Ideas of the Sublime and Beautiful* (1759; Menston: Scolar Press, 1970), pp. 332 and 339.

19 John Gilbert Cooper, *Letters concerning Taste*, 3rd edn. (London, 1757), pp. 2–3.

20 Henry Home, Lord Kames, *Elements of Criticism*, 11th edn (1762; London: Thomas Tegg, 1840), pp. 33–7. For a selection of critics see *Eighteenth-Century Critical Essays*, ed. Scott Elledge (Ithaca: Cornell Univesity Press, 1961).

III Drama

1 Jeremy Collier, *A Short View of the Immorality and Profaneness of the English Stage* (1698; Menston: Scolar Press, 1971), preface and p. 1. For the replies of Vanbrugh and Congreve, see *A Short Vindication of The Relapse and The Provok'd Wife (from Immorality and Prophaneness)* (London, 1698) and *Amendments of Mr. Collier's False and Imperfect Citations, &c, The Dramatic Works of William Congreve*, II, 1773, pp. 235–6.

2 Samuel Johnson, 'Congreve', *Lives of the English Poets* (London: Oxford University Press, 1912), II, p. 29

3 *The Works of the Late Aaron Hill*, 2nd edn (London, 1754), II, pp. 351–2. *Memoirs of Richard Cumberland Written by Himself* (London, 1807), I, p. 81.

4 Allardyce Nicoll, *A History of English Drama 1660–1900* (1927; Cambridge: Cambridge University Press, 1969), III, p. 171. For other views, see John Leftis, Richard Southern, Marion Jones

and A. H. Scouten, *The Revels History of Drama in English*, V, *1660–1750* (London: Methuen, 1976) and Ernest Bernbaum, *The Drama of Sensibility 1656–1780* (Boston: Ginn & Co., 1915).

5 An example is Paul E. Parnell, 'The sentimental mask', *PMLA*, LXXVIII, December 1963, pp. 529–35.

6 Susanna Centlivre, *Letters of Wit, Politicks, and Morality*, ed. Abel Boyer (London, 1701), Letter 39.

IV Poetry

1 *Representative Verse of Charles Wesley*, ed. Frank Baker (London: Epworth Press, 1962), hymn XXIII.

2 For a development of this argument, see Madeleine F. Marshall and Janet Todd, *English Congregational Hymns in the Eighteenth Century* (Lexington: University of Kentucky Press, 1982).

3 For a fuller account of the contrasts, see Stephen D. Cox, *The Stranger Within Thee* (Pittsburgh: University of Pittsburgh Press, 1980).

4 Hoxie Neale Fairchild, *Religious Trends in English Poetry* (New York: Columbia University Press, 1939), I, p. 521.

5 *James Thomson and David Mallet, Miscellanies of the Philobiblon Society* (London, 1857–8), IV, p. 30.

6 For further discussion of this theme, see Fairchild, *Religious Trends in English Poetry*; John Barrell, *English Literature in History, 1730–1780: An Equal, Wide Survey* (London: Hutchinson, 1983); and Louis I. Bredvold, *The Natural History of Sensibility* (Detroit: Wayne State University Press, 1962).

7 Ann Candler, 'Reflections on my own situation . . .', *Poetical Attempts* (Ipswich, 1803).

8 James Macpherson, *Fragments of Ancient Poetry* (Edinburgh, 1760), p. 40.

9 Hugh Blair, *A Critical Dissertation on the Poems of Ossian, the Son of Fingal* (London, 1763).

10 *The Poems of Thomas Gray with a Selection of Letters and Essays* (London: J. M. Dent, 1917), p. 234; 'On poetry in general', *Complete Works of William Hazlitt*, ed. P. P. Howe (London: J. M. Dent, 1930), V, p. 18.

V Fiction: Samuel Richardson

1 See John J. Richetti, *Popular Fiction before Richardson: Narrative Patterns 1700–1739* (Oxford: Clarendon Press, 1969).

2 For the life of Richardson, see T. C. Duncan Eaves and B. D. Kimpel, *Samuel Richardson: A Biography* (Oxford: Oxford University Press, 1971). Richardson is of immense importance in French as well as in English literature, the two having a symbiotic relationship in the eighteenth century. In France the sentimental novel developed at about the same time as in England, notable landmarks being Marivaux's *La Vie de Marianne* (1736–42) and the novels of Crébillon fils, for example *Les Égarements du coeur et de l'esprit* (1736), both translated into English. In mid-century, the French sentimental novel was greatly influenced by Richardson and Sterne, while, towards the end of the century in England, Rousseau and Riccoboni became important models.

3 *Pamela, or Virtue Rewarded* (London: J. M. Dent, 1938), 2 vols.

4 The first edition of *Clarissa* is reprinted by Penguin (Harmondsworth, 1985). The third edition is substantially followed in the J. M. Dent edition (London, 1932). Because I am concentrating on Richardson's efforts to control reader response, references are to the Dent edition unless otherwise indicated.

5 For some of the discussion over the novel, see Jocelyn Harris's introduction to *Sir Charles Grandison* (Oxford: Oxford University Press, 1972).

6 *Selected Letters of Samuel Richardson*, ed. John Carroll (Oxford: Clarendon Press, 1964), p. 83.

7 For Richardson's efforts to control his text, see M. Kinkead-Weekes, *Samuel Richardson: Dramatic Novelist* (London: Eyre Methuen, 1973), and S. Van Marter, 'Richardson's revisions of *Clarissa* in the second edition', *Studies in Bibliography*, 26, 1973, and 'Richardson's revisions of *Clarissa* in the third and fourth editions', *Studies in Bibliography*, 28, 1975.

8 *The Complete Letters of Lady Mary Wortley Montagu*, ed. Robert Halsband (Oxford: Clarendon Press, 1965–7), III, p. 97.

9 *Boswell's Life of Johnson*, ed. George Birkbeck Hill (Oxford: Clarendon Press, 1964), II, p. 175.

10 A fuller version of this argument occurs in my article, '*Pamela*: or the bliss of servitude', *British Journal of Eighteenth-Century Studies*, 6, 2, Autumn 1983, pp. 135–48.

11 Samuel Jackson Pratt (Courtney Melmoth), *Emma Corbett or the Miseries of Civil War* (1780; London: R. Baldwin, n.d.), II, pp. 116–17.

VI Fiction: The Man of Feeling

1 Sir Walter Scott, *Lives of the Novelists* (London: Oxford University Press, 1906), p. 170.
2 Sarah Fielding, *The Adventures of David Simple* (London: Oxford University Press, 1969).
3 Laurence Sterne, *A Sentimental Journey through France and Italy* (London: J. M. Dent, 1960).
4 *Letters of Laurence Sterne*, ed. L. P. Curtis (Oxford: Clarendon Press, 1935), p. 401; *Sterne: Critical Heritage*, ed. Alan B. Howes (London: Routledge & Kegan Paul, 1974), pp. 185–7 and 216.
5 Henry Mackenzie, *Letters to Elizabeth Rose of Kilravock*, ed. Horst W. Drescher (Munster: Verlag Aschendorff, 1967), pp. 16 and 50.
6 Laurence Sterne, *The Life and Opinions of Tristram Shandy, Gentleman* (Oxford: Oxford University Press, 1983), p. 492.
7 Oliver Goldsmith, *The Vicar of Wakefield* (London: Oxford University Press, 1974), p. 21.
8 Adam Smith, *Theory of Moral Sentiments*, ed. D. D. Raphael and A. L. Macfie (Oxford: Clarendon Press, 1976), p. 40.
9 See R. S. Crane, 'Suggestions toward a genealogy of the "Man of Feeling" ', *The Idea of the Humanities* (Chicago: University of Chicago Press, 1967).
10 Examples include Rufus D. Putney, 'Laurence Sterne: Apostle of laughter', *The Age of Johnson: Essays presented to Chauncey Brewster Tinker* (New Haven: Yale University Press, 1949), and R. F. Brissenden, *Virtue in Distress* (London: Hutchinson, 1951), pp. 218–42. Samuel H. Woods Jr. describes some irony-based views in '*The Vicar of Wakefield* and recent Goldsmith scholarship', *Eighteenth-Century Studies*, 9, 1976, pp. 429–43.

VII Fiction: The Woman of Feeling

1 Henry Mackenzie, *Julia de Roubigné* (London, 1777), p. 111.
2 May Sinclair, 'A defence of man', *English Review*, July 1912, p. 559.
3 Elizabeth Helme, *St Margaret's Cave or the Nun's Story* (New York: Arno Press, 1977), II, p. 87.
4 Lady Echlin, *An Alternative Ending to Richardson's 'Clarissa'*, ed. Dimiter Daphinoff (Francke Verlag Bern, 1982), p. 172.

5 Mary Wollstonecraft, *Mary, A Fiction* (New York: Schocken Books, 1977).
6 Sir Walter Scott, *Lives of the Novelists* (London: Oxford University Press, 1906), p. 173.
7 Mary Hays, *Memoirs of Emma Courtney* (London, 1796), p. 223.
8 *Memoirs of Richard Cumberland Written by Himself* (London, 1807), II, p. 257.

VIII The Attack on Sensibility

1 Helen Maria Williams, *Letters written in France, in the summer of 1790 . . ., Letters from France* (Delmar, NY: Scholars' Facsimiles & Reprints, 1975).
2 Major John Cartwright, *A Letter to the Duke of Newcastle . . . .* (London, 1792).
3 Mary Wollstonecraft, *A Vindication of the Rights of Men, in a Letter to the Right Honourable Edmund Burke* (London, 1790), pp. 105 and 145.
4 Edward Gibbon, *Autobiography* (New York: Meridian Books, 1961), p. 206.
5 For an account of these libraries, see J. M. S. Tompkins, *The Popular Novel in England* (London: Methuen, 1932), and Dorothy Blakey, *The Minerva Press 1790–1820* (London: The Bibliographical Society, 1939).
6 For further examples of the eighteenth-century anxiety concerning the danger of fiction to women, see *Novel and Romance (1700–1800)*, ed. Ioan Williams (New York: Barnes & Noble, 1970).
7 Mary Wollstonecraft, *A Vindication of the Rights of Woman* (Harmondsworth: Penguin, 1975), pp. 81–2.
8 Michel Foucault, *Madness and Civilization* (London: Tavistock, 1977), p. 219.
9 William Godwin, *Enquiry Concerning Political Justice* (Oxford: Clarendon Press, 1971), p. 15.
10 Calhoun Winton, 'The tragic muse in enlightened England', *Greene Centennial Studies*, ed. Paul Korshin and Robert R. Allen (Charlottesville: University Press of Virginia, 1984), pp. 125–42.
11 Arthur Sherbo, *English Sentimental Drama* (East Lansing: Michigan State University Press, 1957), p. vii. See also A. W.

Ward, *A History of English Dramatic Literature* (London: Macmillan, 1899), III, pp. 517–18.

12 F. R. Leavis, *The Common Pursuit* (London: Chatto & Windus, 1972), p. 107; D. J. Enright, 'William Cowper', *Pelican Guide to English Literature*, (Harmondsworth: Penguin, 1957), IV, pp. 391–2.

13 Northrop Frye, 'Towards defning an Age of Sensibility', *English Literary History*, xxiii, 1956, pp. 144–52.

14 *Biographia Literaria, Collected Works of Samuel Taylor Coleridge*, ed. James Engell and W. Jackson Bate (London: Routledge & Kegan Paul, 1983), p. 27.

15 William Blake, *Complete Writings*, ed. Geoffrey Keynes (London: Oxford University Press, 1966), pp. 614, 682, and 630.

16 See Angela Leighton, 'Sense and silences: Reading Jane Austen again', *Jane Austen: New Perspectives* (New York: Holmes & Meier, 1983), pp. 128–41.

17 William Makepeace Thackeray, *The English Humourists of the Eighteenth Century* (London: Grey Walls Press, 1949), p. 185.

18 F. R. Leavis, *The Great Tradition* (Harmondsworth: Penguin, 1962), p. 11.

19 Lady Louisa Stuart, *Selections from her Manuscripts* (Edinburgh: David Douglas, 1899), pp. 235–6.

20 Aldous Huxley, *Vulgarity in Literature* (London: Chatto and Windus, 1930), p. 38.

IX Epilogue

1 Douglas Jerrold, *The Mutiny at the Nore* (1830), preface.

2 D. H. Lawrence, *Lady Chatterley's Lover* (London, 1961), p. 105.

3 Harriet Beecher Stowe, *Uncle Tom's Cabin* (Harmondsworth: Penguin, 1981), pp. 427–8.

Selected Bibliography

Barrell, John, *English Literature in History 1730–1780. An Equal, Wide Survey* (London: Hutchinson, 1983).

Bernbaum, Ernest, *The Drama of Sensibility 1696–1780* (Boston: Ginn & Co., 1915).

Birkhead, Edith, 'Sentiment and sensibility in the eighteenth-century novel', *Essays and Studies*, 11, 1925, 92–116.

Brady, Frank, '*Tristram Shandy*: Sexuality, morality, and sensibility', *Eighteenth-Century Studies*, Fall 1970, 41–56.

Braudy, Leo, 'The Form of the Sentimental Novel', *Novel*, 7, 1, 1973–4, 5–13.

Bredvold, Louis I., *The Natural History of Sensibility* (Detroit: Wayne State University Press, 1962).

Brissenden, R. F. *Virtue in Distress* (London: Hutchinson, 1951).

Brissenden, R. F. (ed.), *Studies in the Eighteenth Century* (Canberra: The Australian National University Press, 1968 and 1976).

Butt, John and Carnall, G., *The Mid-Eighteenth Century* (Oxford: Clarendon Press, 1979).

Caroll, J. (ed.), *Samuel Richardson. A Collection of Critical Essays* (Englewood Cliffs, NJ: Prentice-Hall, 1969).

Cash, Arthur Hill, *Sterne's Comedy of Moral Sentiments: The Ethical*

Dimension of the Journey (Pittsburgh: Duquesne University Press, 1966).

Clifford, J. L. (ed.), *Eighteenth-Century English Literature. Modern Essays in Criticism* (London: Oxford University Press, 1967).

Cox, Stephen D., *The Stranger Within Thee* (Pittsburgh: University of Pittsburgh Press, 1980).

Cragg, Gerald R. (ed.), *The Cambridge Platonists* (New York: Oxford University Press, 1968).

Crane, R. S., 'Suggestions toward a genealogy of the "Man of Feeling"', *The Idea of the Humanities* (Chicago: University of Chicago Press, 1967).

Doody, Margaret Anne, *A Natural Passion* (Oxford: Clarendon Press, 1974).

Dussinger, J. A., *The Discourse of the Mind in Eighteenth-Century Fiction* (The Hague: Mouton, 1974).

Eagleton, Terry, *The Rape of Clarissa* (Oxford: Blackwell, 1982).

Eaves, T. C. D. and Kimpel, B. D., *Samuel Richardson. A Biography* (Oxford: Oxford University Press, 1971).

Elledge, Scott (ed.), *Eighteenth-Century Critical Essays* (Ithaca: Cornell University Press, 1961).

Erametsa, Erik, 'A study of the word 'sentimental' and of other linguistic characteristics of eighteenth-century sentimentalism in England', *Annales Academiae Scientiarum Fennicae*, Ser. B (Helsinki, 1951).

Fairchild, Hoxie Neale, *Religious Trends in English Poetry* (New York: Columbia University Press, 1939).

Foucault, Michel, *The Order of Things* (London: Tavistock, 1970).

Foucault, Michel, *Madness and Civilization* (London: Tavistock, 1977).

Foucault, Michel, *The History of Sexuality* (London: Allen Lane, 1978).

Friedman, Arthur, 'Aspects of sentimentalism in eighteenth-century literature', *The Augustan Milieu: Essays Presented to Louis A. Landa*, ed. Henry Knight Miller, Eric Rothstein and G. S. Rousseau (Oxford: Clarendon Press, 1970).

Frye, Northrop, 'Towards defining an Age of Sensibility', *English Literary History*, XXIII, 1956, 144–52.

Hagstrum, J. H., *Sex and Sensibility: Ideal and Erotic Love from Milton to Mozart* (Chicago: University of Chicago Press, 1980).

Hilles, F. W. and H. Bloom (ed.), *From Sensibility to Romanticism* (New York: Oxford University Press, 1965).

160   *Sensibility*

Karl, Frederick R., *A Reader's Guide to the Development of the English Novel in the Eighteenth Century* (London: Thames and Hudson, 1975).

Kinkead-Weekes, Mark, *Samuel Richardson. Dramatic Novelist* (London: Methuen, 1973).

Laslett, Peter, *The World We Have Lost* (New York: Charles Scribner's Sons, 1965).

Leftis, J., Southern, R., Jones, M. and Scouten, A. H., *The Revels History of Drama in English, V, 1660–1750* (London: Methuen, 1976).

Lonsdale, Roger (ed.), *The Poems of Gray, Collins and Goldsmith* (London: Longman, 1976).

Lovejoy, A. O., *The Great Chain of Being* (Cambridge, Mass.: Harvard University Press, 1936).

Marshall, Madeleine and Todd, Janet, *English Congregational Hymns in the Eighteenth Century* (Lexington: University of Kentucky Press, 1982).

Miller, David, *Philosophy and Ideology in Hume's Political Thought* (Oxford: Clarendon Press, 1981).

Miller, Nancy K., *The Heroine's Text. Readings in the French and English Novel, 1722–1782* (New York: Columbia University Press, 1980).

Monk, Samuel, *The Sublime: A Study of Critical Theories in Eighteenth-Century England* (1935; Ann Arbor: University of Michigan Press, 1960).

Nicoll, Allardyce, *A History of English Drama 1660–1900* (Cambridge: Cambridge University Press, 1969).

Nicolson, Marjorie Hope, *Newton Demands the Muse* (Princeton: Princeton University Press, 1946).

Oates, J. C. T., *Shandyism and Sentiment* (Cambridge: Cambridge Bibliographical Society, 1968).

Parnell, Paul E., 'The sentimental mask', *PMLA*, LXXVIII, December 1963, 529–35.

Perry, Ruth, *Women, Letters, and the Novel* (New York: AMS Press Inc., 1980).

Price, Martin, *To the Palace of Wisdom: Studies in Order and Energy from Dryden to Blake* (Carbondale: Southern Illinois University Press, 1964).

Richetti, John J., *Popular Fiction before Richardson: Narrative Patterns 1700–1739* (Oxford: Clarendon Press, 1969).

Rogers, Katharine, *Feminism in Eighteenth-Century England* (Urbana: University of Illinois Press, 1982).

Sherbo, Arthur, *English Sentimental Drama* (East Lansing: Michigan State University Press, 1957).

Sitter, John, *Literary Loneliness in Mid-Eighteenth-Century England* (Ithaca: Cornell University Press, 1982).

Starr, G. A., ' "Only a Boy": Notes on sentimental novels', *Genre*, 1977, 501–27.

Stone, Lawrence, *The Family, Sex and Marriage in England 1500–1800* (Harmondsworth: Penguin, 1982).

Tanner, Tony, *Adultery in the Novel* (Baltimore: Johns Hopkins Univesity Press, 1979).

Todd, Janet, *Women's Friendship in Literature* (New York: Columbia University Press, 1980).

Tompkins, J. M. S., *The Popular Novel in England* (London: Methuen, 1932).

Ward, A. W., *A History of English Dramatic Literature* (London: Macmillan, 1899).

Watt, Ian, *The Rise of the Novel* (Harmondsworth: Penguin, 1972).

Williams, Ioan (ed.), *Novel and Romance 1700–1800* (London: Routledge, 1970).

Williams, Raymond, *The Country and the City* (London: Paladin, 1973).

Wright, Walter Francis, *Sensibility in English Prose Fiction 1760–1814: A Reinterpretation* (New York: Russell and Russell, 1937).

Index